G000123671

Taylor's Gold

Life and times
of a golfing superstar

A Royal North Devon Golf Club Publication

First published 2010
Edward Gaskell *Publishers*
The Old Gazette Building
6 Grenville Street
Bideford
Devon
EX39 2EA

isbn (10) 1-9067696-25-7
isbn (13) 978-1-906769-25-3

© Royal North Devon Golf Club

Taylor's Gold

Life and times of a
golfing superstar

All rights reserved. No part of this publication may be reproduced, stored in a
retrieval system, or transmitted in any form by any means electronic, mechanical,
photocopying, scanning, recording or
otherwise, without the prior written permission of the publishers.

Typeset, printed and bound by
Lazarus Press
Caddsdown Business Park
Bideford
Devon
EX39 3DX
www.lazaruspress.com

This book is dedicated to the
memory of John Henry Taylor

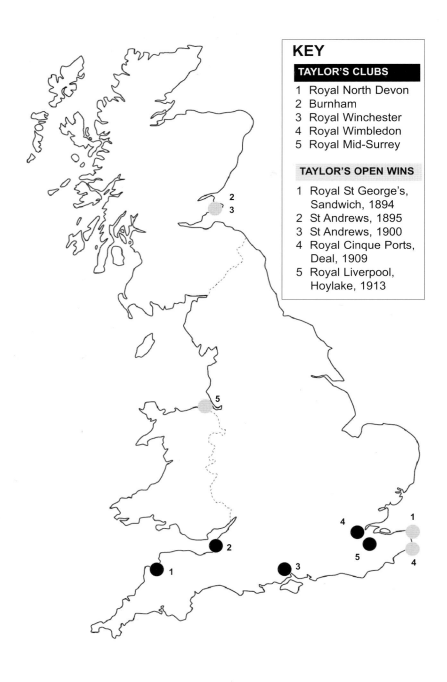

KEY

TAYLOR'S CLUBS

1 Royal North Devon
2 Burnham
3 Royal Winchester
4 Royal Wimbledon
5 Royal Mid-Surrey

TAYLOR'S OPEN WINS

1 Royal St George's,
  Sandwich, 1894
2 St Andrews, 1895
3 St Andrews, 1900
4 Royal Cinque Ports,
  Deal, 1909
5 Royal Liverpool,
  Hoylake, 1913

CONTENTS

INTRODUCTION

THIS book charting the life and times of John Henry Taylor has been published by the Royal North Devon Golf Club to raise funds for a major programme of events leading up to its 150th anniversary in 2014.

The book not only seeks to acknowledge the astonishing achievements of RND's most famous son but also to offer a tangible flavour of JH Taylor the man and the era in which he bestrode the world of golf.

To this end, the club is indebted to the Taylor family for allowing access to his autobiography, *Golf: My Life's Work*, published in 1943 by Jonathan Cape.

It is particularly grateful to Judith and Roger Plumtree, and John Taylor - three of his grandchildren - for their fascinating insights into life with the great man away from the fairways.

The club makes no apologies for delving deeply into Taylor's own recollections - written without the assistance of a ghost-writer - because, nearly 50 years after his death, they still offer the best perspective on what it took to become, and remain, a true giant of the game.

The authors hope that JH's words, coupled with their own research and some - hopefully - intelligent guesswork, will add significantly to your appreciation of one of Britain's genuine sporting superstars.

John Henry Taylor's ascent to the pinnacle of golf was an incredible journey - Royal North Devon Golf Club invites you to enjoy the ride.

WORDS: Jim Hopkins / PHOTOGRAPHY: Patrick Noonan

A MESSAGE FROM PETER ALLISS

A HUNDRED and fifty years of golf on the links of Royal North Devon at Westward Ho! Doesn't that have a wonderful ring to it?

Nobody really knows where the game of golf began: what we do know is that it has been played fairly seriously for about 500 years, but who knows whether many years before that the Romans or their like were playing some form of 'stick and ball' game?

What we do know is the links of Westward Ho! is one of the oldest organised golfing venues in the world, made all the better by its association with one of the Great Triumvirate, JH Taylor. I met him on several occasions and always marvelled at how he had managed to stay with the times, even though he was from a very different age.

I have made several visits to Royal North Devon over the years and have always been enchanted by what I found - apart, perhaps, from the spiky bulrushes that could give the unwary a nasty wound!

One particular memory is of a match played between myself, Max Faulkner, Christy O'Connor and Brian Huggett. If memory serves me right, O'Connor and Faulkner were wearing golfing attire from the early 1800s, and Huggett and I were armed with every modern appliance known to man. Some subtle handicapping went on but, suffice to say, the 'old brigade' won the day, which caused great merriment and a huge amount of pleasure.

Royal North Devon Golf Club is a very special place, and it will, God willing, remain so for many more years to come.

Peter Alliss

JH TAYLOR: THE TRIBUTES

THE ROYAL AND ANCIENT GOLF CLUB OF ST ANDREWS

THE achievements of the Great Triumvirate are well documented. From 1894-1914 they won The Open Champ-ionship sixteen times between them, Harry Vardon a record six times and JH Taylor and James Braid five times each. In these same years, they played more exhibition matches than any of their contemporaries - Vardon played 544, Taylor 529 and Braid 526. The high figure is hardly surprising. Spectators wanted to see the best players in action and once a professional had established his reputation by winning The Open, he could look forward to a lucrative series of invitations to compete in exhibition matches.

John Henry Taylor won his first Open title in 1894 and his fifth and final in 1913. A span of nineteen years separated the two, a record which stands to this day and is a testament to the enduring strength of his game.

In his appropriately titled autobiography *Golf: My Life's Work*, Taylor describes the accolade given to himself, Braid and Vardon as 'a pedestal of such eminence that it was scarcely fair to the rest of our fellow-professionals'. The book reveals a character humbled by the praise bestowed upon him, recognising that the successes of the Triumvirate 'may have been due to the chances and fortunes inherent in an uncertain game'.

Perhaps inevitably, with the passing of time, the Triumvirate has come to be regarded as a single entity. *Taylor's Gold* looks to redress the balance, introducing us to Taylor the man; someone with his own personality, style, interests and ambitions.

Taylor's playing career reveals only one facet of his persona. In 1902 he wrote *Taylor on Golf: Impressions, Comments and Hints*. Not only does it cover the technical aspects of the game, it provides the reader with an invaluable contemporary account of golf. Often frank in his observations of how professionals in golf were treated, compared to those in other sports, Taylor advocated fairness and equality and was keen to encourage changes which would benefit younger up-and-coming golfers.

The values he lived by are values we can relate to today and we are truly fortunate that such a man played our game.

Peter Dawson,
Secretary, The Royal and Ancient Golf Club of St Andrews

THE PROFESSIONAL
GOLFERS'
ASSOCIATION

IN THE Spring of 1901, the letter written by a North Wales golf professional to *Golf Illustrated* may well have had heart-felt intentions, but little did he realise just how significant a proposal he was putting forward, the consequence of which would still be in place today over a century later! In subsequent correspondence the writer would urge JH Taylor to lead the movement of forming an Association to look after the needs of the golf professional.

For that development of foresight we need look no further than "JH" - as Taylor was affectionately known. It is fascinating to comprehend, when reading the various articles about the great man's inner belief, that the golf professional had to be better cared and provided for from the outset of their careers in the game. This principle formed a path from which he rarely deviated.

Bernard Darwin remarked in his introduction to JH's autobiography that "he always had sympathy with those less well off than himself. The institution of the Professional Golfers' Association, with its benevolent fund, the encouragement of Working Men's Golf Clubs and the increase in public golf courses, represent three branches of a movement into which he had thrown all his formidable energies."

And so, in 1901, the Association began with just 59 Members. Today the Association, of which I am honoured to be Chairman, numbers over 7,500 full Members and Assistants servicing the game of golf across all corners of the globe. How would JH have viewed this remarkable transformation and growth of his beloved Association that he set about forming with James Braid and Harry Vardon way back in the Autumn of 1901?

I believe that JH would be justifiably proud of the efforts that have been made on behalf of so many golf professionals in the subsequent years. His own humble beginnings, initially on the greenkeeping staff at Westward Ho!, gave him an extraordinary opportunity to work in areas of the game that today many would quietly decline as being irrelevant to their development. Those early experiences would positively direct his thinking and understanding of the role of the golf professional, a vocation he wholeheartedly embraced

By 1891, JH had moved to Burnham-on-Sea as greenkeeper-professional and further opportunities opened up for him at Winchester and Wimbledon before he arrived at Mid-Surrey, where he would make a very special name for himself.

At Winchester, JH would record two Open titles with victories in the 1894 and 1895 Championships at Sandwich and St Andrews respectively before repeating those triumphs at St Andrews and Deal in 1900 and 1909 playing out of Mid-Surrey. His final Open Championship victory was at Hoylake in 1913 while still based at Mid- Surrey. Rich times indeed!

However, these victories were gained at a cost because JH was now realising that with the impending outbreak of war his time would be split between playing and his club responsibilities.

JH was quickly discovering the one truism today that the true club professional is no longer able to balance the time needed to perform both duties to the highest level of competence.

This realisation gave JH one additional factor of immense satisfaction - and that was simply to give something back to the game that gave him so much. By being the Association's first Chairman he acted as a motivating force to ensure debates and disputes were heard in fair fashion and helped to influence their outcome to the benefit of all within the Professional game.

In his time as Chairman, amongst the many challenges he would oversee was the development of the golf ball from feathery to gutta percha and then, progressively, to the Haskell rubber-cored ball. Similarly, but not until the mid-1920s, he would be asked to intercede in the debate over the use of steel shafts in the manufacturing of golf clubs as opposed to the hickory shafts already in place - these were difficult times indeed for the club professionals of that era but JH's foresight and influence progressively won the day.

JH's unfailing desire was to help drive the Association forward. In so doing, perhaps we can reflect upon words that perfectly encapsulate his belief that "The Professional Golfers' Association's influence, I maintain, has always been towards safeguarding the game its members are happy to serve. I am proud to have helped to build it."

We could all do well to remember that as we start each working day.

Phil Weaver,
Chairman, The Professional Golfers' Association

THE CHILL FACTOR

1

'ONCE you've felt the cold chill of poverty,
it is something you never forget.'

FOURTEEN haunting words that go to the very core of one man's remarkable rise from a barren backwater of rural North Devon to a place in golfing immortality.

John Henry Taylor did not forget.

The suffering of his parents during a desperately impoverished childhood was for ever etched in his soul.

It fuelled his resolve that their sacrifices - and courage - should never be in vain.

Those fourteen words - spoken to a granddaughter by a man not often given to excessive sentimentality - encapsulate the inner forces that propelled him to five Open Championship triumphs.

They help to explain how the boy from the caddie shack who left school before the age of 11 became a revered, radical and articulate administrator who not only campaigned for the rights of his fellow professionals but also championed the cause of golf for all the working classes.

They help to explain how the "urchin" in cast-off clothes came to mingle with monarchs and stand tall among statesmen, sporting peers and celebrities who sought his advice and company.

JH Taylor didn't just have to beat the best players in the world to take his place in the highest echelons of the game.

He also sought to win over the elitists who fought to maintain the sport as the preserve of the privileged and the rich.

And, above all, he first had to break free from the deprivation of life in late 19th century Northam.

The story of his ascent to greatness is both stark and inspirational.

Materially, the Taylor family weren't just poor - they were very poor.

But once you've felt the cold chill of poverty. . .

HOME: The house in Castle Street, Northam, where John Henry Taylor was born in 1871

HARD TIMES

2

T HE WORLD that greeted the arrival of John Henry Taylor on March 19, 1871, had been brutally harsh on his parents. Life for Joshua and Susannah Taylor in the latter half of 19th century North Devon was an unremitting - at times desperate - fight for survival.

For them, affording even the most basic essentials of everyday existence stretched the family budget to breaking point. The much-needed economic upturn in the area, fuelled in part by a surge in tourism and new construction projects, came too late to improve their impoverished plight.

So while, as in any household - however destitute - the latest addition to the Taylor family was a just cause for joy and celebration, in reality the mood around 22, Castle Street, Northam, was one of no great optimism and even less expectation.

As the man who was destined to achieve golfing immortality wrote in his autobiography 72 years later: "The house I was born into was, from the material point of view, a very poor one, the home of an ordinary Devon labourer worthy of far more than the miserable pay that he earned.

"Both of my parents, I am proud to say, had ambitions for themselves and aspirations for their offspring far above their lowly state, but, as they found themselves, there was little hope of either being realised."

Despite the hardship, the family tried to remain upbeat and there does not seem to have been the slightest hint of self-pity at the capricious cards that life had dealt them.

CLASS ACT: JH excelled at Northam Infants School.   PICTURE COURTESY OF DAVID GALE

Taylor recalled in a magazine interview later: "My parents slaved for their children's welfare. They both had high ideals, a horror of anything petty or spiteful, a love of books and an intense admiration for education and all it implies.

"When my brothers and I were busy at nights at our home lessons, I remember gratefully the pride that possessed my parents if our industry was pointed out to any neighbours that chanced to come by."

Far from being intimidated by his background, young John Henry - the second son of five children - appears to have blossomed. At the village school, he proved to be a bright, attentive pupil who mastered every test placed in front of him, and away from the classroom and his family chores, the nearby Northam Burrows offered one of the finest playgrounds any adventurous youngster could wish to encounter - complete with a golf links that was home to the Royal North Devon club.

These were heady days for the young man and his friends - sun-drenched summers or storm-tossed winters alike - and the roots of his love affair with golf were planted around that time.

"I do not know how old I was before I became aware of the fact," Taylor wrote later, "but as soon as I became aware of anything, golf had entered into my life."

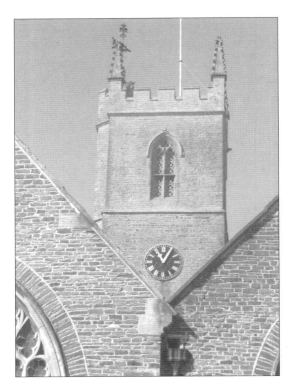

HANDY: The tower of Northam church was the perfect alarm clock for Joshua

But these distractions - welcome though they were - could not mask the deprivation that, in truth, was felt by many of the 4,430 residents registered in Northam, Westward Ho! and the nearby fishing village of Appledore in the 1881 population census.

His parents worked tirelessly to provide their family with the best life they could muster, but all too often they were swimming against the tide.

Joshua, a big, bearded, bear of a man, was a popular figure around the area's building sites, turning his hand to quarrying, sinking wells or general labouring. He was also an employer's dream, believing in a fair day's labour even if the "fair day's pay" did not always reflect his efforts.

At times his dedication to duty verged on the obsessive. JH, who dearly loved and respected his father, later recalled part in awe but also with some incredulity how, because there was no clock in their

SIMPLY THE BEST: JH adored his mother Susannah, above, and vowed to repay the sacrifices she and his father, Joshua, had made for the family during a tough upbringing in Northam

ONE heart-breaking moment in his teens left an indelible mark on Taylor. JH recalled the incident many years later while working on a book with his friend, Harold Begbie.

Begbie, a distinguished writer and poet, had asked JH whether he ever felt any bitterness about his family's plight.

In the darkness of the car, Begbie said it was impossible to see his companion's face, but JH spoke very quickly as he replied:

Yes, perhaps there was a little bitterness. I'll tell you an incident of those days. During one of the worst of my father's illnesses, worst because it was the longest, every penny of our savings was exhausted, and my poor mother was in debt to all the tradesmen. She knew that even when my father was well enough to earn money it would be many months before she was out of the tradesmen's debts.

Well, it was a bitter winter and our little cottage for want of coal was like an ice-house. Hunger made us colder still. It's my belief my mother was eating scarcely enough to keep body and soul together.

We were all shivering and wretched and hopeless. Round came the coalman. "Will you trust me for another hundredweight?" asked my mother. The coalman replied: "I'm sorry, Mrs Taylor, but till you pay for what's owing I can't let you have any more." My mother said "I quite understand", thanked him and shut the door.

There she stood for a moment, just like a statue. I heard the wheels of the coal cart going up the street and presently the cry of the man in the distance. The only other sounds to be heard were the crash of the waves on the shore and the scream of the wind around our little home.

Then I saw something I had never seen before. My mother bowed her face, covered it with her hands, and cried. God in heaven, it was so awful a sight, my brave mother weeping, that I wept too. Yes, there was bitterness in my heart that dark cruel afternoon. It couldn't be otherwise.

J.H. Taylor: Or The Inside of a Week, by Harold Begbie, was published by Mills and Boon in 1925.

cottage, Joshua would wake in the middle of the night and saunter across the village square until he could see the church clock tower and then return to bed - all to ensure that he was the first man to arrive on site for work in the morning.

Perhaps inevitably, the intensity of his commitment was to be his downfall. Employed on the demolition of the ill-fated new pier at Westward Ho! in 1880 - it had been wrecked by storms - Joshua was involved in an accident.

Eager to get the job done, he was working solo on a winch that apparently should have been a two-man operation and the injuries he sustained only compounded the general ill health that would keep him house-bound for the last few years of his life.

By now the family could no longer afford the rent of two shillings and sixpence a week (12.5p) on their modest cottage in Castle Street, and they were forced to take another, cheaper property near the stench and harrowing sounds of the local slaughterhouse.

In an era when no work meant no pay, the impact of Joshua's worsening health dealt a hammer blow to the family finances - and the misery was complete when, with John Henry just 15, Joshua passed away at the age of 46.

He had, in the words of his doctor "worked himself to death", and his son wrote later: "I have been more than fortunate in my profession, but my one regret is that my father did not live to see me become a champion golfer. He died before I could contribute anything towards his material comfort, but I am happy to believe that I never caused him any great worry."

John Henry's mother, Susannah, herself plagued by a chronic back problem that caused her to walk with a stoop, took on the mantle of head of the family.

She was already eking out the family income "at the wash-tub" - washing, scrubbing and ironing for anyone with the money and inclination to employ her - and, as Joshua's health deteriorated, she had been obliged to seek the last resort of "parish pay", a donation from the church, to help make ends meet.

Somehow, despite everything, Susannah still found the time and energy to help the local doctor tend the sick, acquiring enough knowledge along the way to become the area midwife.

Susannah was a kindly, hard-working soul who was quick to praise and encourage but also not afraid to dispense the appropriate dose of discipline if any of her offspring stepped out of line.

JH simply adored her. "Mother was a strict disciplinarian, not harsh but always just," he later wrote in tribute. "When she spoke or ordered, there was no mistake regarding what was required.

"She also possessed an old-world courtesy which demanded that the utmost consideration be paid to everyone, irrespective of class or social status.

"After my father's death, the sight and thought of my poor mother struggling along to keep the roof over our heads was a never-ending pang; I can scarcely restrain my tears when I think about it, and I am not ashamed.

"She fought the world and its evil thrusts with pluck and fortitude and never asked for any quarter. It cut deep down in my soul and determined me, if I were given the strength, to prove worthy of her sacrifice.

"Dear, tender-hearted, courageous and long-suffering mother. Nothing that I can possibly say can repay the debt of gratitude that I owe to one who bore so much for her family's sake. She possessed a dignity of mind and person, an innate sense of the fitness of things, and a nobility of purpose in everything that she undertook. I am happy in the thought that, perhaps, I have inherited a few particles of these traits."

If John Henry felt he struggled to express his gratitude in words, he certainly made up for it in deed.

He modestly omits to mention the fact in his book, but as soon as his fortune began to match his fame as an Open champion, he bought his mother a cottage of her own in North East Street so that she could live out the rest of her days in the village in the comfort she deserved. Susannah was in her Eighties when she died in 1922.

DECISIONS, DECISIONS. . .

3

B Y 1882, the Taylor family had a decision to make, though, in all honesty, it was not a difficult one. Young John Henry had made such impressive progress at school that he had reached the "sixth standard" ahead of schedule at the age of 10.

Under the latest legislation, their son's success in attaining that level of learning presented his parents with two options: either JH could leave school immediately he attained the standard and seek employment, or he could continue with his education on a part-time basis until he reached 13.

Critics of the new law feared that it could open the door for unscrupulous parents to exploit their children in the jobs market. For the Taylors, nothing could have been further from the truth. In their financial circumstances, they simply had no choice but to seek the cash injection that JH's earnings would bring.

So it was that young John Henry, who had been a part-time "bag carrier" on Saturdays and holidays from the age of eight, headed full-time for the caddie shack at the Royal North Devon Golf Club.

But not before fulfilling his less exciting, but certainly more reliable and rewarding daily duties as a "boot boy".

Taylor's description of the job needs no further clarification: "My life as a regular caddie now commenced, but my early mornings were occupied in a less precarious manner. Boot boy - cleaning boots and knives, chopping sticks and filling and carting indoors scuttles of coal - was one of the recognised sources for supplementing incomes. The pay, 2s 6d per week (12.5p today), plus breakfast, was the standard emolument and I must have had half a dozen jobs of this sort to employ my time two hours or so every morning from 7.30 to 9.30, Sundays excepted."

Among those employers was a General Hutchinson, whose son, Horatio - "Horace" - was to become one of the country's leading amateur golfers, winning the Amateur Championship in 1886 and 1887, as well as earning a reputation for being a respected commentator on the sport.

On first impressions, the Hutchinsons personified the class divide that characterised the vast majority of golf clubs of that era, in which an elitist mix of gentry, clergy, the military and schoolmasters fought to maintain a stranglehold on the game they considered to be their exclusive domain.

But the family, showing a more liberal streak, took an instant liking to their part-time employee. Horace wrote in his book, *Fifty Years of Golf:* "It was during my time at Oxford that there came to Wellesbourne (his home in Northam) a little, singularly white-flaxen-haired boy from Northam village. . . I do not know exactly what the duties of an 'odd boy' are, but you may be very certain that he

MENTOR:
Horace Hutchinson took the young JH under his wing. . . and the protege learned so quickly he would score two crucial victories over his 'tutor'

CADDIE CREW: JH, centre, leaning on club, with some of his chums at Westward Ho!

performed them very efficiently when I tell you that his name was John Henry Taylor. He used to do the jobs like a champion."

Horace regularly used JH as a caddie when he was home and, quick to recognise his burgeoning talents as a player, took him under his wing with support and advice - for which JH was eternally grateful.

But first, back to the caddie shack, where the scene appeared to be one of unbridled chaos.

The story goes that the early breed of bag carriers, resplendent in red jackets, had been whipped into shape with military precision by an ex-sergeant major.

JOHN HENRY TAYLOR has only the haziest recollection of his earliest days on the links. He told *Golf Illustrated* in 1905 that he couldn't recall when he started playing, only that "I cannot remember when I did not play golf."

He had managed to cobble together "a mere apology for a set of child's clubs" and dedicated himself to perfecting his game.

There is no record in Taylor's autobiography that he received any formal tuition, but we do know that Johnnie Allan, Royal North Devon's first professional and one of three Scottish brothers attached to the club, had a major influence on him.

Taylor wrote: "His size and geniality were magnets that drew me towards him. Of course, Johnnie knew of my poor circumstances and to this fact I attributed his many kindnesses.

"Later on, when I became a regular caddie, I learned to appreciate Johnnie's finer qualities, and from him I learned many things which fixed my ambition to become a golf professional."

It seems inconceivable that, as his talent shone through, Taylor was not offered some form of coaching from people like Horace Hutchinson or succeeding RND club professionals, Willie Dunn and Charles Gibson.

He might also have shared some time on the links with a young Rudyard Kipling, who was to achieve his own fame as author of *The Jungle Book, Stalky & Co* and the poem *If* among many other notable works that would earn him the Nobel Prize for Literature.

Kipling was a pupil at the United Services College for gentlefolk at Westward Ho! from 1878 to 1882 - Taylor would have been between the ages of seven and 11 and Kipling five years older.

When Taylor later wrote to inform the writer of the death of a mutual acquaintance, Kipling replied expressing his sorrow, and adding: "Those were the days when the Burrows were free to all and, as you remember, we golfed where and when we chose, and there were very few books or theories to confuse the mind or the muscles."

If that was the case, then there had been a serious breakdown in discipline by the time the young Taylor took up his post.

Fred Karno's Army might be a more accurate description of the "lawless and undisciplined hordes" - Taylor's words - that populated the caddies' tin hut.

With no rotas in operation, the helter-skelter scramble when a potential "bag" made his way to the first tee was matched only by the speed of the vanishing act when a more troublesome client came into view.

Taylor, by his own admission, was not the quickest on his feet and regularly floundered at the back of the pack as his fitter and stronger colleagues dashed to offer their services.

Even when he did finally claim the prize, it might easily have ended in tears.

Because of an eyesight problem, Taylor failed to spot where his client's ball had landed after a wayward shot disappeared into thick rushes.

His paymaster, Major Hopkins - "Shortspoon" of artistic fame and an irascible character on the golf course - immediately docked him half his fee, so his "reward" for the four-and-a-half hour round was just 3d (marginally more than 1p today).

He might have taken umbrage, but instead accepted the pay cut as a lesson learned. Anyway, he had just pocketed his first-ever earnings from golf - and the look of sheer delight on his mother's face when he presented her with the money more than made up for the shortfall.

But as the weeks passed, the RND members began to realise there was perhaps something different about this wee lad known as "Wig" because of the colour of his hair.

He was a quick and willing learner of the caddie's art and, more importantly, conducted himself with a dignity that made him very popular with his golfing masters.

Taylor, for his part, realised at an early stage that a day on the fairways listening to the opinions and experiences of his successful clients could help to compensate for the education he had forfeited by leaving school so early.

He later wrote in a magazine article: "I soon found out that prospective employers were influenced by other things than the quick covering of the ground. I had made a name for civility and attention to duties and, though I might lag behind and come up breathless to offer my services, I was employed more often than not.

AN ORIGINAL PHOTOGRAPH OF SOME OF THE MEMBERS
OF THE NORTHAM ARTISAN GOLF CLUB 1888

1. WILLIAM HUTCHINGS.	8 WILLIAM FULFORD	15 CHARLES COWLER	22 THOMAS GEEN
2 HARRY WILLIAMS.	9 SAMUEL FULFORD.	16 WILLIAM WORTH	23 ERNEST CAWSEY
3 WILLIAM DAVIS.	10 HARRY STEVENS.	17 WILLIAM PURSEY	24 RICHARD BURCH
4 BERTIE WAY	11 SIDNEY DIAMOND	18 GEORGE CANN	25 CHARLES COOK
5 JOHN ROWE.	12 EDWARD LABBETT	19 JOHN HENRY TAYLOR	26 JESSE BRAUND
6 WILLIAM HEARN	13 JOHN HUTCHINGS.	20 THOMAS METHERALL	27 LEWIS CHAPELL
7 THOMAS GLOVER.	14 RICHARD DAVIS	21 WILLIAM PUNCHER.	28 JOHN PENHORWOOD

PRESENTED TO THE CLUB BY JOHN ROWE 1938

26

THE FORMATION of the Northam Working Men's Golf Club in 1888 - the first of its kind in England to offer golf for the less privileged - proved to be an important stepping stone for the young JH.

With a membership drawn largely from ex-caddies not short of their own skills, the club provided the impetus for its best players to hone their skills in a competitive environment.

John Henry, then 17 and playing off scratch, relished the challenge. He won the club's premier competition, the Gold Medal, in 1888, and repeated his triumph the following year playing off plus-two.

He later wrote: "The realisation of this success brought with it a thrill that can only come to a youngster on the threshold of fresh, inspired hope. It proved to my colleagues and myself that I was perhaps gifted with the ability to knock a ball about with greater skill than they, who were no mean critics."

"A caddie's life is a great educator. If he is willing to learn and shows an intelligent desire to try to improve his mind and his vocabulary, he has plenty of opportunities to do so. I am afraid that my anxiety to keep close to the heels of my employer was prompted not so much by the endeavour to please as by a wish to listen to any conversation and to learn what was going on in the large outside world."

There were other, more immediate golfing lessons to be learned.

Taylor wrote: "I carried for all and sundry, but I must confess I had my favourites. I had a leaning, like all caddies, towards the low handicap players, not because their service was more remunerative since it was generally the reverse, but because by watching I could pick up tips that could become useful."

For four years, the young JH rejoiced in his caddie life "as only a carefree urchin can, revelling in the open-air existence, making full use of every hour, whether employed or idle."

But now was the time for change.

Club rules decreed that all caddies should hang up their bags at the age of 15 and search for more permanent employment. Taylor accepted the ruling, "but only with much heart-burning and not a little resentment."

The problem now was: what next?

Not golf, it would seem - at least not yet.

His first job was as a gardener's boy for "a very remarkable man, Captain W Blakeney of the Royal Navy, who was kindness itself to me", but the worsening financial situation at home forced him to look for a better-paid position.

By now Taylor had a hankering to join the Services or the Metropolitan Police.

Amazingly, with the degree of hand-eye co-ordination required at any level of golf, let alone to win five Open Championships, he was rejected by the Army five times because of his short-sightedness and once, by the artillery, for having flat feet.

To add salt to his wounds, the Royal Navy - despite a glowing reference from Capt Blakeney - dismissed his application to become a stoker because at 19 he was too young, and the Met Police turned him down because at 5ft 8in he failed to meet their minimum height requirements by one inch.

No wonder he was moved to remark ruefully when the final rejection landed on his doorstep: "It seemed that Providence had destined me for something less bloodthirsty than soldiering and more exciting than shovelling fuel into a warship's interior."

His aspirations to enlist in the Services dashed, Taylor began to look more closely to home for ways to support his mother.

The options were limited, so it was no surprise when he turned to his father's old trade of labouring to bolster the family budget.

The hours were long - 6.30am to 6pm with half an hour for breakfast and one hour for dinner - but the rewards of 15s a week (75p) were a substantial improvement on his wages as a gardener.

There was another positive, too. Taylor wrote: "Carrying bricks and mortar in a hod up ladders is not an inspiring job and it also has the disadvantage of being very hard work. But I have no doubt that it greatly helped to build up my strength and develop my physique into something like manliness."

This extra power brought a new dimension to his fast-improving golf game - and soon there would be opportunities to put it to the test.

The first came in 1889 when a group of top Scottish and English professionals arrived in Westward Ho! for a tournament to celebrate RND's 25th anniversary - and Taylor, along with a few other local ex-caddies, was invited to make up the numbers.

Taylor wrote: "Such a galaxy of golfing stars had not been gathered together in the south of England before and their coming was of special interest."

He survived the first hurdle, beating the young Bob Kirk, before falling victim to Archie Simpson in the second round.

The significance of the tournament was not the victory over Kirk - though, indeed, it was a creditable scalp - but that it brought him into contact for the first time with Andrew Kirkaldy, one of the day's leading professionals. Kirkaldy, as will be revealed later, was to become a major factor in Taylor's rise to prominence.

Taylor stuck to the task of labouring for almost 18 months - he was particularly proud of his contribution to the scheme to widen Bideford Quay - until, out of the blue, came an offer that was to change his life.

By the beginning of 1889, the Royal North Devon club were looking to replace a member of their groundstaff who had died during a particularly savage winter.

Perhaps influenced by the impression he had made as a caddie and the improving skills he was now showing as a player, Dr Siddall, the chairman of the Greens Committee, and the then club professional, Charles Gibson, had no hesitation in recommending Taylor for the position.

JH wrote: "It was an opportunity that I never dreamed would come my way and when it did I was overjoyed at the thought of what it meant. I was back on the links doing a job I loved, a club in my hands every spare moment and gaining a rudimentary knowledge of greenkeeping which later on was to prove the basis of further improvement."

With more time to practise, Taylor's game continued to thrive and he had another chance to showcase his skills in 1889 when the Northam Working Men's Golf Club, formed the previous year, was challenged to a match against a team representing Royal North Devon.

Inevitably, as the Working Men's leading player, Taylor was drawn against none other than his mentor, Horace Hutchinson.

"I am bound to confess that I viewed the match with some misgiving as Horace was considered to be unbeatable," JH wrote in his book, "but my work on the links had enabled me to put a polish on my game and I was not afraid."

He had no need to be, winning his match two up on the final hole.

The result was a huge shock to the Royal North Devon members and one told him after the match: "That was a great triumph, Taylor, but you will never do it again!"

That, as we shall discover in due course, would prove to be a false premise.

For his troubles, Taylor also earned a rebuke from the RND secretary, the Rev IH Gosset, at the after-match awards.

JH had been tarring bunker shuttering on the morning of the match and had not had time to change out of his working clothes before his tee-off time. The secretary took umbrage that Taylor was still wearing the overalls at the presentation ceremony - but he didn't know that Taylor possessed only one other pair of trousers, his Sunday best. . . and they were for Sundays!

The incident quickly forgotten, Taylor spent two extremely happy years tending the links at Westward Ho! before the opportunity for "further improvement" mentioned earlier arrived a little sooner than perhaps he had imagined.

A new golf club had been formed in Somerset and they were offering him the position of greenkeeper-cum-professional.

Another crucial decision was required, one that addressed the age-old dilemma of the young, particularly those who had never stepped outside the sheltered environment of a rural community like North Devon.

The new job carried a wage of 18s a week (90p), four shillings (20p) more than he was earning at Westward Ho! But what if he didn't make the grade in his new post - he'd lose the 18s and his old job would almost certainly have been given to someone else. Do you take a gamble on forfeiting a job you love in an area where you are comfortable for the possible promise of something better in a town you don't know?

Taylor wrote: "It was a serious and anxious problem that I had to face. I argued like this. I had a job that in all probability would last me a lifetime. Was it wise to chuck it for the dubious prospect of making good in another that carried a more direct responsibility? It sounds silly now, but it meant much heart-searching for me then."

If he truly was agonising over the dilemma, it was quickly resolved for him

His mother, Susannah, had no doubts about the wisdom of accepting the new challenge - and backed her judgment by borrowing a sovereign to send him on his way.

So with a pound in his pocket and armed with a large wooden chest that contained his worldly possessions, on January 1, 1891 John Henry Taylor took the first steps on a journey that was to lead to golfing greatness.

HAVE BOX, WILL TRAVEL: The wooden chest with which JH set out on his epic journey

BUOYANT AT BURNHAM

4

IF THE FIRST PART of that journey, 60 miles up the Bristol Channel to Burnham-on-Sea, represented something of a gamble for both parties, then any worries were swiftly banished: everyone proved to be a resounding winner.

Taylor's fears that it might be a step too far, too soon, quickly evaporated as he thrived on the responsibilities of his post. For him, it was "new and inspiring", the perfect introduction to life as a golf professional.

For the recently-formed Burnham club, the success of Taylor's tenure was a total vindication of the faith that its founding father, Canon Charles Kennard, had placed in the raw 19-year-old.

Kennard, a Roman Catholic priest, had identified land among the sand hills at nearby Berrow Warren as a location rich in potential for a golf course. After that assessment was confirmed at a site meeting with Charles Gibson, the professional at Royal North Devon, the Burnham club was formally inaugurated in October, 1890.

On the recommendation of Gibson and Kennard, the post of greenkeeper-cum-professional was offered to John Henry Taylor.

In his book *Between the Church & the Lighthouse* - a history of the Burnham and Berrow club - Philip Richards wrote: "The choice of JH Taylor was inspirational. Not initially for his golfing ability, because at that time he was a good but young and improving player, but for his enthusiasm and hard work in preparing the course and getting it ready for play so quickly."

That was no mean feat. The original course, laid out by Gibson over nine holes and measuring around 2,300 yards, was bedevilled by swathes of sand whipped up in near Saharan proportions by winds that swept along the Bristol Channel coastline.

Taylor's first major task was to implement a long-term programme of planting, seeding and turfing to protect the fairways from the ravages of the sands. Burnham's huge reputation today is due in no small measure to his skills and endeavours.

Taylor also had another role to play, though it had not been in the original job specification and it was not one that he consciously pursued.

Many among the good, but poorer, village folk of Berrow had strongly resented the 'hijacking' of their warren by their more prosperous neighbours from Burnham and were not averse to acts of vandalism to make their point.

Perhaps because of his own deprived background, Taylor quickly became the idol of the young boys from Berrow and in his book Richards acknowledged the "important part" that Taylor had played in helping to restore harmony between the communities.

These were happy days for the young John Henry, who recalled: "The distance from a groundsman to professional bridged a great chasm, and I walked across with no little trepidation. I might be a decent greenkeeper, but I was not so sure of becoming even a tolerable professional. But I fell among friends who gave me every encouragement to perfect my game and were good enough to predict that the brand of my game was good and only needed the chance of competition in order to reveal itself."

One such opportunity had arisen at the formal opening of the Burnham club in June, 1891, when he once more faced his old "friendly" foe Horace Hutchinson. The young man prevailed three and two, exploding the myth of the North Devon member who had proclaimed two years previously that "it would never happen again".

Another chance came in 1892 and would not only provide a career-defining victory but also, in mildly bizarre circumstances, spell the end of Taylor's 18-month sojourn at Burnham.

Canon Kennard, president at Burnham, had set up a challenge match between his man, Taylor, and the professional at Winchester, where the priest's brother, Adam, was also president.

The match was to be played home and away with a bounty of £12 for the winner donated by members of both clubs.

BERROW BOY: JH takes to the links during his spell at Burnham as greenkeeper-professional

The professional at Winchester - on a short-term secondment of six months - was the legendary Scot Andrew Kirkaldy, whom Taylor had first met when he played in a tournament alongside a galaxy of top golfers at Westward Ho! in 1889.

Kirkaldy, beaten in a play-off for the Open Championship in that same year, was still one of the leading players of his generation, but he came second best to his young rival.

Taylor considered himself fortunate to be only one down after the first 18 holes at Winchester, but mastered the sand hills and intricacies of his home course so clinically that he closed out the match four and three.

"I realised that by winning I had set my foot on the long ladder that might enable me to climb to great heights," he wrote later of his first challenge match victory.

A more immediate outcome was that Kirkaldy, who had already decided to return to Scotland just six weeks into his stint at

ANDREW KIRKALDY was a fearsome competitor not noted for his magnanimity in defeat.

So when JH took the spoils in their Burnham v Winchester challenge match it was surely cue for a tempestuous tirade against the golfing gods for betraying him in his hour of need.

Not a bit of it.

To almost universal surprise - not least to JH himself - the volatile Scot walked off the last green, linked arms with his rival and said, without a trace of rancour: "Well done, laddie, by God, you're a guid gowfer."

The story doesn't end there.

Mocked mercilessly by his

Scottish peers on his return home for losing to the "wee Englishman", Kirkaldy, now livid with rage, rounded on his detractors with the warning: "I'm telling ye, yon Taylor is a graun gowfer and would tak' the breeks off all of ye."

Which, very loosely paraphrased, meant: Ignore him at your peril, the lad can play.

Taylor never forgot Kirkaldy's act of sportsmanship after their match and the pair began a friendship that would last until "Andra's" death in 1934.

Winchester, recommended Taylor as his replacement, a view that the hierarchy of the Hampshire club was quick to endorse.

Much has been made of the fact that Taylor gave no reason for leaving in his resignation letter to the Burnham committee, but it did nothing to sour a relationship that had been hugely beneficial to both sides. Taylor continued to return as a willing visitor and Burnham always received him as a welcome guest - none more so than in 1926 when a very proud father went back to his old club to watch his eldest son, John - known as Jack to most of the family - make his debut for Oxford University in the first of his three Varsity matches against Cambridge.

THE LEGEND of JH Taylor lived long at Burnham. His achievements inspired no fewer than 18 young men from Berrow to follow in his professional footsteps in the fledgling days of the club.

In particular, two golfing dynasties, both born in the shadows of the village church, came to prominence - the Whitcombes and the Bradbeers.

Taylor had left Burnham before they began to make their mark in the game, but there is no doubting that his aura as an Open champion and the encouragement he offered on return visits to the club provided all the stimulus they needed in their careers.

Charles Whitcombe would take part in seven Ryder Cup matches as a player or captain between 1927 and 1949 and was selected for the 1939 contest before the outbreak of World War Two.

His brother, Ernest, appeared in three Ryder contests, while a third brother, Reginald, who won the Open at Sandwich in 1938, played in 1935 and had also been picked for the 1939 team.

In a sibling feat that surely will never be repeated, all three were selected for the 1935 match at Ridgewood Country Club, in Paramus, New Jersey.

The impact was much the same on the Bradbeer clan, who provided the professional at Burnham for an unbroken 60-year spell between 1919 and 1979.

From a family of 14 - four were girls and one brother died young - nine became professional golfers. Famously, four of them - James, Bob, Ernest and Fred - all qualified for the final two rounds of the 1928 Open at Royal St George's.

Burnham, it seemed, took the view that Taylor's departure was simply a matter of an ambitious man who had become a very good golfer seeking to maximise the opportunities of an excellent offer when it arose.

Taylor's explanation, revealed in his book, was that his frustration at a never-ending battle against the sand was the overriding factor in his decision to quit Burnham.

In truth, both were probably correct.

Taylor wrote later: "I was now fairly launched on the turbulent seas of a professional golfer's life - turbulent because its navigation is not easy, neither is it possible to escape the reefs of disappointment.

"I could see before me a life of moderate comfort and, in contrast to my earlier struggles for a living, a degree of affluence, and I was determined that nothing should be wanting on my part to secure both.

"Providence had given me a means of earning my living that was at once the most agreeable and best fitted to my ambition, and I should count myself a sorry knave if I abused it by unworthy conduct. Many men I saw did so, but this only made me the more resolved not to err from the line of sobriety and to avoid anything debasing."

Taylor was now clearly a man with a plan. More competitive matches would further hone his skills as a golfer; the rapidly-expanding circuit of challenge matches around the home counties would help to swell the coffers.

London was the place to be - "it had a pull for all professionals who desired to get to grips with the heart of things" - and although Winchester was not the ultimate destination, at least it was a large step in the right direction.

Once you've felt the cold chill of poverty. . .

WONDERFUL WINCHESTER

5

S O IT WAS that in October, 1892, John Henry Taylor swapped life in coastal Somerset for the more bustling city of Winchester, the capital of Saxon England.

Taylor instantly warmed to its old-world ambience and the four years he spent there were some of the happiest of his life.

Winchester Golf Club had been formed at Morn Hill only four years earlier - it gained "royal" status in 1893 - and perhaps a realistic pointer to its standing in the community at that time was the fact that the club's competition and match results were published in the society page of the local newspaper, not the sports columns.

No-one could have foreseen that within three years the members would have a double Open champion in their midst.

Taylor's original appointment as club professional, like that of Andrew Kirkaldy before him, had been for just six months, but he reasoned that through hard work and strength of personality he could persuade the committee to make the post permanent. Not for the first time, his instincts proved correct.

Taylor wrote: "The gamble came off. At the end of the six months, and greatly to my delight, I was offered a whole-time position which gave me a sense of greater security. I began to think of the possibility of founding a home of my own.

"Winchester's quiet and cultured atmosphere, the college, the barracks, its many churches dominated by the magnificent cathedral, the old city redolent of early English history, it all captured my imagination from the first."

He particularly embraced the life of Winchester College, which boasted its own golf course, and his friendship with the masters there - 'Teddy' Buckland, "who hit the ball further than anyone I

HAMPSHIRE CHRONICLE,

Basingstoke, Andover, Alton, Alresford, Southampton, and Isle of Wight Courier,

AND GENERAL ADVERTISER FOR THE SOUTH AND WEST OF ENGLAND;

CIRCULATING IN THE COUNTIES OF HANTS, SUSSEX, SURREY, BERKS, WILTS, DORSET, AND SOMERSET.

THE OPEN GOLF CHAMPIONSHIP.—For the second time the English golfer, J. H. Taylor, professional t the Royal Winchester Golf Club, has won the ope championship, for on Thursday he repeated at St Andrews the victory which he gained at Sandwich last year. Taylor as well as English golfers generally may well be proud of the result, and the members of our local club will no doubt highly congratulate him on his arrival home. On Wednesday the first day's play took place in fairly favourable weather. The competition is by strokes, four rounds of the green (or 72 holes in all), the competitor totalling the lowest score to be declared champion for the ensuing year. The pick of English and Scotch amateurs and professionals started, Douglas Rolland, of Rye, being,

SMALL TALK:
The local newspaper, *The Hampshire Chronicle*, can't be accused of overplaying JH's second Open victory at St Andrews in 1895

ever saw"; the Rev Trant Bramston, for whom "arrayed in oilskins and sou'wester, no weather was too bad to deprive him of his afternoon round"; or Dr Rendle, who later became the Head, "for the fright he used to give me when riding his penny-farthing bike up and down the steep hills" around the city.

Taylor revelled in the atmosphere - and it did not take him long to make a mark of his own.

He won his first Open Championship at Sandwich in 1894 and further stamped his footprint on the golfing world by repeating that triumph at St Andrews the following year.

The Sandwich victory sparked a huge boost to Taylor's profile - and his earning power.

The diary began to bulge with requests for personal appearances and the challenge matches that were a crucial component of a professional golfer's income.

Taylor wrote: "My Championship win put me in great demand for exhibition matches. It would serve no useful purpose in giving the names of my opponents or the results. But the monetary rewards I received from them added to my bank balance in a substantial manner, which I carefully preserved, remembering that my tenure of the high position might be short-lived, and it was prudent to make whatever hay I could whilst the sun of prosperity shone."

OIL FINERY: Graphic artist Tom Branton, then a Winchester member, spent more than a hundred hours in1994 researching and creating his original painting in oils to commemorate the centenary of Winchester professional JH Taylor's first Open win at Sandwich. Tom now plays at High Post, closer to his home. The above montage forms part of a collection of memorabilia in the JH Taylor Room at Royal Winchester.   PICTURE COURTESY OF TOM BRANTON

AS AN Open champion, JH Taylor was in much demand, but there was one date that he was never going to miss - one that "the winning of a Championship was but a minor episode by comparison."

In April 1895, in Easter week, he married his fiancée, Clara Fulford, at St Mary's Church, in Bideford, North Devon.

He wrote: "I had known Clara for many years when, as a callow boy, I went snooping into Bideford casting googlish eyes at all the maidens in the hope that one would take pity on me. Clara eventually did.

"Whatever my merits or demerits as a husband, her courage in facing the rough and smooth that life brings, her cheerfulness and devotion to home life and children, the constant and loving help given me in all my worries and anxieties have been such as to cause me to wonder whether a better wife has ever existed."

The couple moved to Winchester and were to have nine children. Tragically, a son, Kingsley, and daughter, Jeannie, died in infancy while another daughter, Cicely passed away in her twenties. The remaining children were Dorothy, Marjorie, John, known to most of the family as Jack, Leslie and the twins, Phyllis and Audrey.

That is not to say that he deserted his duties at Winchester.

His coaching prowess had greatly improved standards of play at the club and he was thrilled when one of his pupils, Miss Amy Pascoe - who made the not inconsiderable journey from Woking for her lessons - won the Ladies' Open at Hoylake in 1896.

He was also instrumental in introducing a golf club manufacture and repair facility to Winchester.

Previously, the work had been out-sourced to a sports shop in the city, causing a loss of profit to Taylor and minor inconvenience to Winchester's members.

Taylor looked for ways to bring the operation back in-house - and the problem was solved when his old friend, George Cann, completed his apprenticeship as an assistant professional at Royal North Devon.

The pair, both ex-caddies, had grown up together in Northam and Cann, who had forged an excellent reputation as a club-maker during his time at Westward Ho!, jumped at the chance to join his pal at the Hampshire club.

Using some of Taylor's money, some borrowed by Cann, and a helping hand from the Winchester committee, who built them a

CLUB CALL: JH, second from right, lines up with some of the members at Winchester

workshop, Cann & Taylor, club manufacturers, burst into business in October, 1894.

It proved to be a fruitful partnership - more of which later - but, for one potential customer at least, the title name of the company was to cause some confusion in the ecclesiastical city.

Taylor explained: "One day we received an order for golf clubs. Presumably because we were in Winchester, a city of many clerics, the sender addressed his letter to 'The Rev Canon Taylor' and congratulated the 'Canon' on seeing fit to combine his duties of holy office with those of a purveyor of golf goods."

The business prospered, but by 1896, Taylor had reluctantly reached the conclusion that it was time to leave the city.

As his celebrity rose with more and more matches and engagements, the burden of travelling to and from Winchester increased, so when he discovered that Royal Wimbledon was in the market for a professional, he applied for and was offered the post.

Taylor never lost his affection for Winchester - and he was to return there in 1901 to lay out their new course when the club

42

switched from Morn Hill to a new site across the city at Teg Down. Taylor was against the move, believing Morn Hill had "just settled down nicely", but he conceded that if the club had to relocate, then it could not have picked a better site.

JH wrote: "I was sorry, truly and deeply sorry, to leave Winchester, only consoled with the enduring memory that the four years spent there were among my happiest. I shall remember with profound gratitude the opportunity and privilege afforded me of residing in the ancient city and of being associated, in however humble a capacity, with the College whose proud and challenging motto is "Manners Makyth Man."

ALL SMILES: John Henry with Andrew Kirkaldy, left, and his brother Hugh, centre, at St Andrews in 1895, the scene of Taylor's second Open Championship victory

WIMBLEDON WOE

6

Q UITE SIMPLY, the move to Wimbledon was a mistake. JH Taylor confessed later that his two years there "were none too happy."

Charles Cruickshank, in his *History of Royal Wimbledon Golf Club*, was more forthright. "It was not," he wrote, "a successful appointment."

Taylor was installed as the club's professional in October, 1896, selected from an original list of 55 applicants.

He had been blissfully happy at Winchester, but Wimbledon had its own appeal.

Taylor wrote: "The club's members contained a big percentage of old Scottish players and with such an aroma about it and thinking its proximity to Waterloo Station would save the long journey back to Winchester after matches, I accepted the post."

So where did it all go wrong?

From Charles Cruickshank's account of events, it is hard to see that there could have been any room for ambiguity about the job.

The Wimbledon hierarchy was adamant that club manufacture and repairs and some course maintenance were part of the brief.

Taylor would receive a salary of 20 shillings (£1) a week, a free workshop and showroom for sales and repairs, and free coal and gas.

In return, he would be available to members on the three days a week that play was allowed on the Common and keep in good condition the holes on the course for which the club accepted responsibility - they shared the facility with London Scottish Golf Club.

He must also keep a stock of clubs and a staff of workmen sufficient to carry out all repairs.

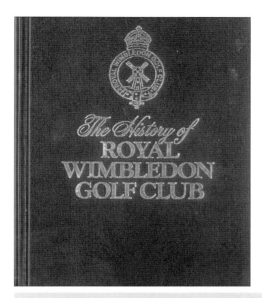

STRAIGHT TALK: Charles Cruickshank, author of *The History of Royal Wimbledon Golf Club*, gives his verdict on JH's spell at the club, below

❛ It was not a successful appointment. Taylor admits, 'My two years at Wimbledon were none too happy owing to causes that I need not explain, but the principal cause of my discontent was the restriction to three days' play a week, which put my earning power at the caprices of the weather, a factor that at all times affects the Professinals' income to an extent that is rarely recognised'. There may have been other causes, but it seems clear from the club records that restriction of earning power was by far the greatest source of discontent. Taylor was cut out to be a tournament Professional, and a showman. ❜

Subject to these conditions, he would be free to do what he liked on non-playing days, but would need to seek special leave for matches away from the course.

From the club's perspective, they quickly felt that maintaining the course was not high on Taylor's list of priorities.

The Greens Committee met him in November, 1897, to express their concerns, but because he had been in charge for only 13 months they gave him the benefit of the doubt.

A year later, according to the club, nothing had changed. Dissatisfaction was now running high, and Taylor accepted an option to renegotiate his contract.

He would now receive no salary, but would be allowed to go absent whenever he chose and continue to be granted free use of the workshop and showroom provided that he maintained a service of club sales and repairs.

Taylor wrote of the sorry saga: "The principal cause of my discontent was the restriction to three days' play a week, which put my earning power at the caprices of the weather, a factor that at all times affects the professional's income to an extent that is rarely recognised."

To be fair to Wimbledon, it does seem a little implausible that a man brought up with the vagaries of the weather at Westward Ho! would not factor this eventuality into his business plan.

So perhaps Taylor's reference to other "causes that I need not explain" held the key to his unrest.

Cruickshank, using club records, confirmed that, yes, Taylor had been concerned about the restriction of his earning power and, yes, "there may have been other causes."

But if he or the club knew what they were, they weren't saying, either.

Perhaps one clue to the problem came with the decision of George Cann, Taylor's business partner, to move to America in late 1898 to develop their club-making enterprise.

Taylor backed the plan, but wrote later: "I'll admit that I felt lost without George. The business was growing. Besides my ordinary duties, I was busily engaged in playing away matches, attending Championships and the like, and the additional responsibility of book-keeping, which I detest, and attending to the many necessary details were sufficient to keep me fully employed. This was not conducive to the maintenance of my playing form, but it had to be done."

Whatever the rights and wrongs of the situation - and there was no lasting acrimony because JH returned to Wimbledon 13 years later to advise them on proposed course changes there - it is fair to surmise that it was a relief to both sides when, in January, 1899, Taylor accepted the chance to become the professional at nearby Mid-Surrey.

MAGNIFICENT MID-SURREY

7

JOHN HENRY Taylor had finally arrived at his destination. The journey from the backwaters of rural North Devon that had begun with such trepidation eight years previously was now complete.

Mid-Surrey - formed in 1892 and accorded royal status in 1926 - was the perfect fit for his ambitions and he was to remain there for almost 50 years

Taylor wrote: "My coming to the Old Deer Park with its pleasant surroundings, its fine turf and the club well established with play every day of the week gave me the feeling that at last I had found a spot in which I could settle down for good and provide the means for bringing up my rapidly-increasing family in decency and reasonable comfort."

The chemistry between "master and servant" was seamless from the start - and much of the credit for that was due to the man-management skills of the Mid-Surrey committee.

At a time when many clubs were keeping their professionals on a tight rein, Mid-Surrey immediately recognised that to get the best from its new man it would have to give him the freedom he needed to pursue his glittering - and lucrative - playing career.

The club's reward for this latitude would not only be the kudos and other more tangible benefits of its association with a multiple Open champion but also the unstinting dedication he brought to the club.

Peter Ryde, in his beautifully-crafted club centenary book, *Characters & Kings, The Making of Royal Mid-Surrey*, wrote: "It is not possible to draw a clear distinction in the context of Royal Mid-

MID-SURREY MAESTRO: This portrait, which also features on the front cover, was created by artist Amanda Fletcher from an original by TM Ronaldson which was destroyed in the fire that ravaged the Royal Mid-Surrey clubhouse in 2001. London-born Amanda says: 'Luckily there was a film of the painting which I could view on my computer and this made the job much easier. There was also a photograph, but I found this less useful.

'Because it is more of a copy than an original work, I am not sure how much credit I can take. But there are, of course, elements of my own style as well. Doing literal copies is rather laborious, so inevitably one does tend to branch off a little and re-interpret certain things.' For more information about Amanda's work, go to www.amandafletcher.net

OPEN FOR BUSINESS: Taylor outside his professional shop at Mid-Surrey

Surrey between Taylor the champion and Taylor the club professional because the club benefited abundantly from the fame he enjoyed and the respect in which he was held as a national sporting figure.

"But, in two respects at least, his contribution to the club is clearcut: the physical changes he wrought in the historic but unpromising piece of land with which he was confronted on his arrival in 1899, and his unswerving loyalty. . .

"The club soon found in him, for all his eminence as a player and his determination not to rest on his laurels, a loyal and conscientious servant, ready to supervise the state of the course and to attend to the needs of a swelling membership."

Mid-Surrey had been prepared to offer its new professional a retainer of up to £2 a week - twice the figure he had originally received at Wimbledon - but in the end both sides agreed that initially there would be no fee and the club would rent him a shed for his professional shop.

IN 1921, JH was asked to take a look at two golfing brothers at Mid-Surrey. He wrote to their father: "They are of two distinct types: Leslie is robust and hard-hitting, whereas Henry is more methodical and careful, and, I should judge, more inclined to know 'the reason of the cause and the wherefore of the why'. Both will do well. Henry will concentrate and go far."

The father's surname was Cotton - and Henry went on to win three Open Championships, in 1934, 1937 and 1948. He also succeeded JH as Royal Mid-Surrey's club professional in 1946.

In reality, Taylor's earnings from club-making, challenge and exhibition matches and the increasing number of tournaments in the golfing calendar would more than take care of any loss of retainer.

JH did lay down one condition, though, that was non-negotiable - as a deeply- religious family man he would not work on Sundays.

Mid-Surrey did not officially recognise Sunday golf, but as long as members did not employ caddies, they were left to make their own decisions about playing. Their professional's stance was not a problem for them.

Taylor quickly settled into his new life at Richmond. He recognised that his record as a double Open champion had played a part in his appointment and was desperate to repay the club with its first Championship winner.

The members did not have too long to wait as Taylor duly obliged with his third Open victory - his second at St Andrews - in 1900.

According to *Golf Illustrated*, the committee was so grateful for the distinction he had brought to the club that Taylor was made guest of honour at the club dinner, at which members showed their appreciation with a staggering collection of £84 18s 9d (approximately £84.95), with lady members contributing a further £10.

Taylor and his family moved into The Lodge, a spacious five-bedroom house within the grounds of the club. It would remain their home for many years until the property was demolished to make way for a road development scheme and they were forced - complete with housekeeper Agnes - to move to another house in Old Deer Park Gardens, Richmond.

Meanwhile, JH threw himself into the day-to-day business of the club, although, as Ryde wryly pointed out, "it will clearly not do to picture him as a domesticated professional standing each morning at the door of his little shop, in his heavy tweed trousers and boots, with three-button jacket to match."

By way of example, *Golf Illustrated* published a list of golfing engagements for all the top players throughout 1904. Taylor's name appeared 43 times, including courses as far apart as Portmarnock, Harlech, Jersey, Hunstanton, North Manchester and - on successive days - Dunbar and Musselburgh, where he won a mouth-watering £130 over both courses.

But, despite his constant travels, he never neglected his responsibilities at home and, in 1910, Taylor and Mid-Surrey's fabled green-keeper, Peter Lees, embarked on a massive and radical re-design of the men's course.

Since its inception, the underlying weakness of the course had been the flatness of the terrain on which it was laid out.

The problem had not been helped when the club - free from some of the restrictions on what they could do with the land - launched into a new but largely one-dimensional programme of bunkering that reached almost epidemic proportions.

The solution for Taylor and Lees was to transform many of these bunkers into a series of "humps and hollows" which are still a feature of the course today.

It took two winters to complete the job, an army of more than 100 unemployed workers toiling to shift thousands of tons of soil with little more than their own muscle-power.

The results of their labours gave a new definition to the course, with many of the "hollows" created in front of greens that had previously been too open.

Describing the principle behind the revamp to *Golf Illustrated* in 1911, Taylor said the obstacles on a golf course should be the "Borstal system" of a golfer's life, teaching him that the way of the transgressor is hard, but not crushing his spirit.

Three years later, writing in his brother Joshua's book, *The Art of Golf*, his sense of achievement had not dimmed when he reported: "Lees and I had the satisfaction of converting a flat, uninteresting

GRACE AND FAVOUR:
JH and England cricket
legend WG often played
together

POWER PLAY: The Aga
Khan was a frequent visitor
to Mid-Surrey for lessons
with JH and the pair
became good friends

course into one that from first tee to last hole is ever changing in character."

He would undoubtedly have taken huge pride in the club's decision in 2010 to name the course he had helped to create a hundred years earlier "The JH Taylor Course".

Taylor's Open victories in 1909 and 1913 brought even greater honour to the club, adding to what Ryde described as the "invisible assets" of their relationship. He wrote: "To the club came friends of his, people in the public eye who would spread the news of John Henry Taylor and his club to a wider audience."

Among the many famous visitors to Richmond were the cricketer WG Grace, The Aga Khan, the entertainer Sir Harry Lauder and boxers Jimmy Wilde and Billy Wells. During the First World War JH, along with many of his professional colleagues, travelled the country to play charity matches in aid of the war effort and for the last six months leading up to the Armistice he worked in the sports department of the Government's Navy and Army Canteen Board, buying and selling equipment for the Services.

Despite his Government "secondment", the Mid-Surrey committee decided that he would remain as the club professional.

Indeed, throughout the war Taylor and a much-reduced ground staff had toiled tirelessly to maintain the courses and it was in recognition of this work and other services to the club that he was made an honorary member in 1920. This honour was upgraded to life membership just before his retirement in 1946.

The partnership between the club and their superstar had indeed been enlightened and special.

Peter Ryde wrote: "It is no small achievement that Royal Mid-Surrey stood behind him, understanding his needs, easing his progress, providing continuity and acting as a sheet anchor during the flowing of a career which, taken all round, is one of the most remarkable in the whole history of the game."

Ryde sub-titled his centenary book The Making of Royal Mid-Surrey.

It is not too far a stretch of the imagination to suggest that the relationship between club and professional was also, in part, The Making of John Henry Taylor.

JH: FAMILY AND FRIENDS

8

JOHN HENRY TAYLOR lived for his family. Nothing mattered more to him. Here, four of his grandchildren offer their recollections of life with the great man away from the fairways.

Some of their observations are family folklore passed down from their parents; others are memories of their own time spent with JH in the latter stages of his life.

Their stories paint a picture of a private man very much of his Victorian age.

They tell of strictness and huge generosity, of integrity and not a little quirkiness.

His late daughter, Phyllis, adds - in her own inimitable style - her tribute to JH in word, hymn and poetry, while the writer, Harold Begbie, brings another perspective with a striking appreciation of his good friend.

Finally in this chapter, JH himself recalls some of the diverse characters he met in the course of his career. . . but nothing, and no-one, meant more to him than his family.

JUDITH PLUMTREE'S home sits high above the Burrows in Windmill Lane, Northam.

The bungalow enjoys a breathtaking vista across the Royal North Devon golf course and the Bideford Bay beyond.

Her grandfather, JH Taylor, described it as "the finest view in Christendom".

JH and his wife, Clara, had bought the property in the late 1930s and originally used it as a holiday home, but when he retired in

PERFECT MATCH: JH wrote: 'I went snooping into Bideford casting googlish eyes at all the maidens in the hope that one would take pity on me. Clara eventually did.' They married in 1895

'The finest view

BAY WATCH: A sea mist rolls in over Lundy Island, but the view of the RND club house in the

in Christendom'

foreground, the Burrows, and Bideford Bay beyond is breathtaking.   PICTURE BY ALAN FALKNER

1946 after 47 years as club professional at Royal Mid-Surrey, the couple moved in permanently.

They were joined in 1954 - two years before Clara's death - by their daughter, Phyllis, and her children, Judith and Roger.

So what are Judith's recollections of the great man?

"Well, he had this aura about him," she said. "Everyone seemed to look up to him, even those who did not know him too well.

"My grandfather was kindly, but very strict. I wouldn't say he was aloof or austere, but private. I suppose he was a typical Victorian man.

"He was head of the family and master of the house. We treated him with respect: what he said went. As a grandchild, you wouldn't pester him.

"But everything he did, he did for the family. Away from golf, family and the church were the two most important things in his life. He went to church regularly and sang in the choir at St Margaret's in Northam as a boy and again after his retirement.

"He was careful with his money, but also very generous. As soon as he could afford it, he bought his mother, Susannah, a decent home of her own in Northam. It was his way of saying thank you for the sacrifices she and his father had made for him.

"In fact, he bought each of his children a home when they married. But it wasn't just immediate family that he cared for. If some of the more distant relatives needed financial help or advice, he would always try to do what he could to solve their problems.

"He wasn't a handyman and employed a housekeeper to help Clara. When he was home, he would usually stay in. He didn't drink or smoke, but occasionally took snuff, much to my grandmother's annoyance. A true Devonian, he arranged for cream and butter to be sent by post to Richmond each week.

"He wasn't one to socialise - he didn't go down to the pub or anything like that - but he would speak to people if they spoke to him first. I suppose he preferred to keep himself to himself.

"Politeness and good timekeeping were very important to him. He felt he should always be polite to people, even those he did not particularly like. But if you were even just a couple of minutes late, he would let you know.

"He was also extremely patriotic - during the First World War he and other professional golfers would travel the country to play exhibition matches without fee to raise money for the war effort. When Singapore fell to the Japanese in 1942, I'm told he hardly spoke to anyone for days. After he retired to Northam, there was no television in the house, and he hardly ever listened to the radio. The nine o'clock news was about the only thing he was interested in. He wasn't one for the arts, either, but he did read books. As you can see from the shelves behind you, he loved the works of Rudyard Kipling and Charles Dickens - *Pickwick Papers* was a favourite. He never owned a car and I can't ever recall him being behind the wheel of one.

"My mother obviously looked after him, although it wasn't that he couldn't take care of himself. But he was devastated when Clara died and I don't think he ever really recovered from that."

Judith, a retired civil servant, added: "There is one particular story I remember my mother telling me about my grandfather.

"A young JH and his mother, Susannah, were walking in Westward Ho! when they were approached by a gentleman from the United Services College in the village who practised the art of phrenology. He told Susannah he could tell the youngster's talents by the shape of his head and rubbing his hands on his skull.

"Susannah let him go ahead, and the gentleman announced: 'Madame, you have a remarkable child there, someone who will make his mark in the world'.

"He certainly got that right, didn't he."

• CLARE BACKWAY lived as a child with her grandparents in Northam during the Second World War.

She frequently asked JH about his childhood and he talked in depth of the harsh circumstances the family faced, especially when his mother was widowed with five children to support. This was when he used the phrase "once you've felt the cold chill of poverty it is something you never forget."

She asked him in later years what he considered to be the most rewarding achievement of his long life and he replied: "Being able to buy the cottage for my mother and knowing that she would not have to pay rent for the rest of her life."

BEACH PARTY: The Taylor family, above, enjoy a day out at Westward Ho!, probably in the early 1910s

BROTHERS IN ARMS: JH strikes a fine pose with William, left, and Joshua. From the shine on JH's shoes, it appears the "boot boy" never lost his touch

BACK SEAT DRIVER: Fellow professional Ralph Smith takes the wheel with James Braid along-side, while Ted Ray, JH and Harry Vardon complete the gang in 1912. Ray won that year's Open
PICTURE COURTESY OF ROYAL MID-SURREY GC

JH TAYLOR was the second son of five children born to Joshua and Susannah. So what happened to the other three brothers and sister?

Robert, the eldest, was born in 1869 and like JH had left school very early, so it was quite an achievement for him to qualify as a teacher. Tragically, he died of pneumonia in 1896, aged just 27.

William, born the third son in 1873, joined the Royal Navy and was on board HMS Montagu when it ran aground in fog on Shutter Rock, off Lundy Island, in the Bristol Channel, during a training exercise in 1897. He wasn't implicated in the court martial that followed the incident, but he would later die in Wolverhampton during the Second World War.

Emily, the fourth child, was born in 1875 and she did what most Victorian girls did - she got married and raised a family.

The youngest, Joshua Jnr, had a particularly colourful career. Born in 1881, he fought in the Boer War, then joined the Royal Flying Corps before eventually following in his brother's footsteps by becoming a golf professional, including a stint at Richmond Park, one of the courses that JH had fought so hard to open for public use. He played in 12 Opens - his best finish was 14th in 1913 when JH clinched his fifth Championship - and, like his brother, published books on golf and was chairman of The Professional Golfers' Association.

Roger Plumtree, a former Royal Marine who later worked in the Navy Department at the Ministry of Defence, wrote this appreciation of his grandfather so that younger members of his family could understand the scale of his achievements. He says that, for reasons of personal sanity, he has never played a round of golf in his life - but that philosophy doesn't detract from his skill in relating his recollections.

"Look on my works, ye Mighty, and despair"

THESE ARE the words of the "king of kings" Ozymandias in the poem of the same name by Percy Bysshe Shelley. They could well have applied to the mere mortals watching my grandfather, John Henry Taylor, in his pursuit of the Open Championship.

Bernard Darwin, the foremost and most eloquent golfing correspondent of the day, put it another way: "My eyes have beheld the glory and I am really and truly sorry for those who can only read about it".

Mr Darwin remained a fan all his life and maintained there was no other golfer he would rather watch than JH, especially if the conditions were thought unfavourable for golf.

Ivor Brown, journalist, author and critic in a later generation, recalled that by diligence as well as by aptitude JH was, from an early age, a master-craftsman.

On JH's departure from Royal Mid-Surrey, Brown presented him with one of his books and penned the following words on the frontispiece: "Something to read beside the Pebble Ridge where were schooled two great men: Rudyard Kipling, unique with the pen, and yourself, unique with a club". A splendid valediction.

To the dismay of many north of the border, JH was the first English professional to break the long succession of triumphant Scots winning the Open Championship, at Sandwich in 1894.

The following year he also won on his first visit to the glory that is St Andrews - a course that initially disappointed JH: he thought it dullish and flat and inferior to his beloved Westward Ho!

Time precludes us from undertaking any accurate assessment of his golfing prowess in comparison with the leading exponents of

PUNCH LINE: The Royal Mid-Surrey club presented this Sir Bernard Partridge cartoon to JH on his retirement in 1946. It first appeared in *Punch* magazine in 1926 and the editor, Sir Owen Seaman, added his own special message, as Roger Plumtree records in his recollections

QUICK ON THE DRAW: Taylor was a main attraction for many of the day's cartoonists, including, left, Spy in *Vanity Fair*; above, celebrating the birth of the "Champion Twins" Phyllis and Audrey in 1909 - the year he won his fourth Open; and, below, another caricature after his victory at Deal that year

TICKET TO RIDE:
JH hitches a lift on a
rickshaw during a tour of
South Africa by a group of
golf professionals in 1936

today. Different eras should not and cannot be evaluated to determine absolutes.

Let us just recall that he played with hickory-shafted clubs and a ball with the aerodynamic properties of laughable content compared with the technological marvels of today. So equipped, he took on his generation of fellow professionals and frequently placed himself at the top of the field, and nothing more can be asked of any professional golfer in any era.

Photographs of the day show him wearing his usual golfing attire of a cap pulled low over his forehead, a loose-fitting linen jacket that buttoned up, a shirt complete with collar and tie, cuffed corduroy trousers and a pair of lace-up leather boots - boots that behoved a one-time "boot boy" - which were always highly polished on every occasion that he ventured on to a course.

But no photograph really did him justice in terms of stature. In them, he appears nothing more than the average height for the time - about 5ft 8in tall. The photographs lied. He was a big little man, a pocket-battleship of a man, possessing a frame that for two years worked as a general labourer. His shoulders were broad - very broad - and he was deep-chested, with well-muscled arms, thick wrists and fingers that, even in his eighth decade, had a vice-like grip.

Once in New York at the turn of the 20th Century, he had been mistaken for a boxer. A huge head completed the picture. It was often described as leonine, with thinning fair hair (almost white) and blue eyes. Like Sir Walter Raleigh, he spoke "Devonish" all his days in a soft, lilting tenor voice.

His strength, allied to his exemplary eye-to-hand co-ordination and ability to judge distance - despite being short-sighted in his left eye - were God-given talents that ensured he never had to continue labouring for his entire working life.

He possessed a firm, flat-footed swing. His mastery lay with the irons, especially the mashie-shot pitched high and straight to the green from any distance within 150 yards, while his putting, resting on thighs like girders and a rock-steady head, ensured mastery of the greens.

His younger brother, William, joined the Royal Navy as a Boy Third Class and in 11 years advanced to become possibly the youngest Warrant Office (Gunner) of his generation. He also

JH disliked left-handed golfers. A letter in *The Times* in 1991 asked why, although 12 per cent of the population were left-handed, so few golfers played that way. Taylor's grandson, Roger Plumtree, responded with this explanation: "I cannot proffer any physiological reasons for the disparity, but I can report the depth of feeling it generated in one of the great teaching professionals of the century.

"Once, in all ignorance, I sought the advice of my grandfather on the subject. Thirty-one years have not diminished my amazement at his response. It was a tirade of rising indignation at the mere thought of sinistral individuals besmirching the beautiful symmetry of his beloved game. Amid the torrent of words I can recall were 'abomination in the sight of the Lord', 'cack-handed nonsense' and the earthy Devonian expression of 'muckers'."

obtained high marks in the increasing severity of specialist training in gunnery and torpedo work.

JH readily accepted the brilliance of his brother and his own shortcomings. "He has more common sense in his little finger than I have in my entire body" was his assessment.

Indeed, his mother's kindly judgment of JH when young was to call him a fond "Tom Fool" and there was much maternal worry as to how his life would pan out because of his natural ham-handedness.

My grandfather was a man of conviction who never adjusted his view to obtain favour: he was resolute to the point of obstinacy.

The Times obituary stated: "There have been among professional players of games many men of character but none perhaps more remarkable than he." When he believed he was unable to compete at the highest level, he immediately retired from competitive golf.

His blue eyes seemed to look into the soul of any individual speaking to him, so direct was his concentration. He taught himself to be a clear, forceful speaker, and he was as efficient with a pen as he was with a club. He lived by routine in everything that he did, and everything he did he endeavoured to do to the best of his ability.

During the "Bodyline" bowling hiatus in Australia in the 1930s, JH wrote to *The Times* suggesting that the term "it isn't cricket" had become so devalued that it should be replaced by "it isn't golf". That conviction remains as true today as when he wrote those lines.

Golf has one specific quality possessed by no other sport. It is a destroyer. It can destroy absolutely or, if the individual is fortunate, it can merely wound.

Professional or amateur golfer, rabbit or old hand, golf will provide an occasion when it will impose itself upon the individual to their total, blood-boiling detriment. Anyone contemplating a career in golf should be made aware that such occasions will - not might - occur.

JH, despite his success at the highest level of the game, was no exception to experiencing such shafts of destruction. His two major incidents were of such magnitude that, on each occasion, JH was adamant a Championship was lost.

It is not an exaggeration to state that these two strokes in his golfing career were those that he relived in his mind at some time during every day of the remainder of his long life.

When asked about his golfing career, he would sit with arms folded and then talk about his experiences in his soft Devon burr, but his talk would invariably arrive at the two shots that had become seared upon his memory.

He would shake his head and grip his hands and then reveal his anxiety by scratching the back of his hands while recalling the moments that produced so much anguish to him.

The first was in 1896 at Muirfield when he was going for a third consecutive Open Championship. In his words: "I see my shot now. It was a hard-hit brassie stroke, but rather low which struck the face of the bunker and dropped in. Had my second shot been a few inches higher my gamble may have succeeded."

That was damaging enough but, although he did not know it at the time, it would prove to be the lesser of the two "hurts".

The other shot was during the Championship "decider" in 1914 against Harry Vardon. The winner would become the first man in history to capture six Open Championships.

Taylor described the shot in his autobiography, *Golf: My Life's Work* as "the greatest tragedy of my golfing life."

It occurred at the fourth hole. Vardon steered his drive splendidly between the hazards that James Braid, only shortly before the Championship commenced, had positioned to make the hole more difficult. JH tried to emulate his friend and adversary but only succeeded in hitting the ball off the heel and it meandered into a shallow bunker at the bend of a stream. His next shot went into the Burn. A lift and drop plus a penalty stroke, and three putts put a seven on his card. Vardon won by three strokes.

JH considered his greatest golf was played on the last morning at the Hoylake Championship of 1913. In what has been described as a hurricane and driving rain, he challenged the elements and went round in 77.

In the afternoon round, he played what he believed was the greatest shot of his career. His drive carried the corner of the garden of the Briar's hole. That stroke was followed by one of his beloved mashie shots which, to those who witnessed it, seemingly cut a hole

COARSE MANAGEMENT: JH was singularly unimpressed by the standard of golf and etiquette shown by the Liberal Prime Minister David Lloyd George, right

in the wind, nearly struck the flag and ended a mere foot or so from the pin.

That club, a mashie, resided in a corner of his study for many years, a proud reminder of the "golden moment" that every golfer dreams about, but seldom attains.

JH was a frequent visitor to many of the great houses of the realm - and continental chateaux - as it was then the vogue for affluent families to hire a golfing professional for tuition and a round of golf.

He took the transference from humble Devon cottage to ducal or royal estate in his stride. The social mores of the age demanded that he would dine off silver plate - alone with the Butler of the Household.

He tutored the then Crown Prince of Japan while he was at Oxford and played many a round with the then Aga Khan in this country and abroad.

It is perhaps unfair to malign those who cannot respond to any assertion of incompetence, but one memory in particular resided in JH's mind - the worst player he ever had the misfortune to play a round with, the Liberal Prime Minister David Lloyd George.

TEACH-IN: John Henry passes on the benefits of his golfing knowledge to sons Jack, left, and Leslie at Mid-Surrey, probably in 1925.   PICTURE: LOVELL SMITH, RICHMOND

I can recall now the note of rising indignation in JH's voice when he talked about his "partner's" antics on a golf course. The tirade embraced a total inability to stand still, a refusal to accept advice, wild uncontrolled swings with every variety of club and turf-breaking akin to mining. It all led to the final condemnation that the individual should never be allowed again on any hallowed golf course.

As a very young child, I once had the honour of being handed his five Championship medals to hold. I was oblivious to the endeavour - physical and mental - that had been expended in gaining such prizes. I know now that men have killed for less while, for the majority of golfers, watching the titanic struggles on the Championship courses of today is the nearest they will get to even seeing such golden gifts from the gods.

In 1900, JH visited the United States and competed in their Open Championship, finishing runner-up to Vardon by two strokes. He told me that his recovery shots produced amazement among the watching audience such was his accuracy. Many of his putts were long and, on four occasions, they rested on the very lip of the cup.

He was taken by the growing popularity of the game there and the enthusiasm for establishing golf clubs and golf equipment concerns. He returned to England with plans to move to the United States to establish himself as a club-maker and course designer and to participate in the fledgling golf circuit there.

His wife, Clara, was unwilling to emigrate and the idea lapsed, but, deep down, JH always considered it was a major opportunity lost.

He visited America again in 1913, finishing tied 30th in their Open, and returned again in 1922 for a number of exhibition matches with Sandy Herd. He captained the 1933 Ryder Cup team and gained immense pleasure from the British victory against Walter Hagen and his golfers.

After 47 years as the professional at Royal Mid-Surrey, JH retired to his bungalow in Northam that overlooks the Royal North Devon Golf Club.

There exists a drawing by Sir Bernard Partridge that was published in *Punch* magazine on September 29, 1926. It is a picture of JH standing fore square in front of the clubhouse at Westward Ho!

A club is tucked under his arm. Beneath it are words by Sir Owen Seaman, the magazine's editor, as a memorial to his prowess as a golfer and as an individual: "Nine tailors must you take to form a man of average degree; 'twould need nine very special men to make another Devon Taylor such as he."

In retirement, he frequently went into his rear garden and just stood staring lovingly at the vista in front of him - the Burrows, with the golf course (the oldest links in England) laid out before him, its attendant complex of sand dunes, the Pebble Ridge and beyond that the golden beach of Westward Ho!, the grey-blue Atlantic Ocean and off centre on the horizon, Lundy Island.

Being able to see such a panorama convinced him it was nature's reward for a man fully contented with life and his personal achievements in a game that once was his work, golf.

• Footnote: JH was my maternal grandfather. My late mother, Phyllis Mary Taylor and late aunt, Audrey, were the "champion twins" (so named by the *News of the World* as they were born in 1909, the year JH won his fourth Open Championship).

JOHN TAYLOR, the third JH, is now retired from a career that included adult education and community action. He has amassed an impressive collection of correspondence relating to his grandfather and here are some of his memories. . .

I WAS born in April, 1940, and so was something short of 23 when my grandfather died. I have clear memories of the old man, but thinking back now I realise that my perception of his character was strongly influenced by various stories my parents told.

As a child I enjoyed my father's occasional tales of his childhood in a large family at The Lodge, most of which are recounted in Aunt Phyllis's memoir.

My father would retell these anecdotes at the tea table, where my brother, sister and I were a rather unruly and argumentative presence.

The story that impressed me most was that of my grandfather's reaction to such indiscipline. As corroborated by Aunt Phyllis, he would reach for a cane that lay along the top frame of a picture hanging behind his head, and in his fury once brought the picture crashing down.

My grandfather was punctilious in listening to the news, both at six o'clock and nine. My mother told the tale that, after the latter, my grandmother would sometimes ask him to leave the radio on so that she could hear the play: but he would always turn it off. My grandmother's one surviving letter to my father reveals, however, that she was able to listen to the daily service.

Once when we were down on holiday - it might have been in 1949 - JH went into the village shop at Northam to buy us children a beachball. He stormed out again when told the price was something like 7s11d (40p). This was another of my mother's stories.

My father always told the anecdote of the cane and the picture with amusement. But the fact was he worshipped JH, even though over time he played down this filial piety in the face of a certain amount of groaning from the rest of the family.

His real feelings are perhaps best expressed in some undated typewritten notes, presumably for a talk he gave, I would say in the 1970s.

"When I was small my incessant cry when I put my head round the kitchen door was 'Where's Dad?' and I have never lost the close-

TAYLOR AND SON: JH with Jack as a tot, probably taken some time around 1907

ness and intensity of this bond. Above all, he was a devoted family man; each one of his surviving children was presented with a house on marriage and he was always asserting that a family life was the most fruitful of human pleasures."

In a typescript memoir written in 1953, my father describes very vividly his own recollection of JH's golf in the latter years of his career. He concludes:

"There can be little doubt of the impress of his character on his style of play. It was accuracy incarnate, decisiveness, definiteness, cleanness, rightness. Other men have expressed their grace or power by their method of striking; every shot that 'JH' played was instinct with clean hitting and what I would call intellectual decisiveness and moral emphasis. To him there was only one way of hitting the ball and that was dead centre or perfectly."

Aunt Phyllis, in her memoir, characterises my father as a "dreysack", a Devon term meaning "impractical dreamer", a view that may well have been shared by other siblings.

Yet JH held him in high regard and affection, even admiration. After a few unhappy years in the tea trade, my father went up to Oxford in 1925 to read English. Here he not only gained a Blue in golf but was elected president of the Junior Common Room at University College, known as Univ, and as such was that year's representative of the undergraduates there.

In the autobiography we read: "Not the winning of any of my five Open Championships pleased me more." It's a statement that seems to me extraordinary, but it testifies to the relationship between father and son.

That relationship comes across in the letters from JH that my father kept.

There are 12 altogether: the first dated 1920 when Dad was recuperating from surgery on his neck, the last three being lettercards from 1961.

Here he is writing to my father just before his Finals in 1928: "A day or two away from the atmosphere of Oxford should enable you to face the examiners with a calm determination. Please do not worry as to the result. Whatever you get will be sufficient to please me as I know you will have tried really hard to obtain the highest."

Later the same summer JH writes to congratulate Dad on winning the Kashmir Cup at Westward Ho!: "Your vivid account of your gallant fight on Sat (sic) fills us all with still greater admiration. It certainly was a case of 'dogged as does it'. Your start was none too good and the disaster at the 5th was enough to shake the most courageous.

"It shows that you are made of the real Devon stuff."

In 1953, just after his 50th birthday, Dad appears to have written a letter of thanks to his father, perhaps in response to a specific gift

FAMILY PRIDE: JH wrote to son Jack, right, congratulating him on his Kashmir Cup success. "It shows," said JH, "that you are made of the real Devon Stuff."

75

or perhaps expressing a more general gratitude. This is also the date of the memoir referred to above.

JH replies: "What we have been able to do for you since the day you blessed us by coming has been done with sincere thankfulness which you have more than amply repaid by your love and devotion during the past 50 years."

I remember these cards and letters arriving in the 1950s, perhaps every ten days, so presumably Dad wrote back with equal regularity. Whether he wrote so often from the beginning of his marriage in 1938, I don't know. In the Fifties, JH would also forward him a weekly golf magazine.

My father, for his part, suffered from a sense of inadequacy in comparison with his father. "Famous men rarely have famous sons," someone had told him early on. Dad was nevertheless a quiet achiever in his chosen field, a headmaster who built up a highly successful state grammar school in suburban Essex. It was a model of excellence in which he took great pride.

My father's relative lack of self-confidence impacted in turn on the next generation. But rather than go down that path, let me relate what I personally recall of my grandfather.

My memories cover the period 1949-1953 when I was between nine and 13 and he was either side of 80. I was impressed by the old man and proud of him. I also greatly enjoyed the good-humoured bustle that other visiting family members brought into the house, which was crowded with golfing pictures and memorabilia.

My sharpest memories date from 1953, and come from two directions that I have difficulty putting together. I remember firstly the photograph listed as "Cuttings Scrapbook 12" being taken in the front garden in Windmill Lane.

It shows a smiling JH flanked by my father and three middle-aged visitors. I had come down with just my father for a week. We stayed at a bed-and-breakfast near Bloody Corner, and over several days I trailed glumly along as he and the three visitors played foursomes round the course at Westward Ho!. Who the others were I don't know: they weren't friends of my father.

Research shows this was also the year in which Lindsay Hassett captained the visiting Ashes team, though in my mind I had put it earlier. The first four matches were drawn but amid great excitement England won the final Test. I remember sitting on the sofa in Windmill Lane cutting out the cartoon narrative of the previous day's play at the Oval that appeared each morning in, I think, *The Express*, the cartoonist perhaps Roy Ullyett.

My grandfather would look on benignly. When I wasn't reading about cricket or glancing furtively at the *News of the World* I was reading the opening chapters of the autobiography - the "immortal work" as JH called it with jocular solemnity as he handed it to me. He was proud of it, and pleased that I enjoyed reading it.

I would describe him then as an imposing figure: somewhat hunched but with powerful shoulders still and a commanding nose and chin, and in between a cropped bristly moustache. I picture him always in a cap.

What impressed me most, I think, was his gruff, clipped, heavily-accented Devon speech. Harold Begbie, in his book, gives a lot of verbatim quotations from JH about playing better golf and how games might regenerate the nation. To me, they don't ring entirely true, being too voluble: the result (I suspect) of Begbie boiling down their conversations into monologues. As I remember it 30 years later, his usual way of speaking was much closer to that of his radio tribute to Harry Vardon, of which I have a recording - that is to say, measured and slightly rhetorical.

I would say: "We're going to the beach this afternoon, grandpa." (Aunt Phyllis had a beach-hut behind the Pebble Ridge at Westward Ho!) "Yes," he would usually reply, "that's right, my boy. Go and immerse your vile body in the pure ocean."

JH combined this formality of speech with great courtesy of manner, something my mother - not an entirely positive witness, as we saw - always acknowledged with appreciation.

My grandmother, Clara, was a gentle, self-effacing presence. I remember her sweet smile and her soft Devon voice. She addressed JH as "Father".

For my father, she knitted socks. I remember them arriving regularly. I would say Dad took her rather for granted.

That summer of 1953 was, I'm pretty sure, the last time I saw JH, and such are my rather paltry memories.

JH's daughter, Phyllis, an international rower, would almost certainly have represented Great Britain at the 1940 Olympics but for World War Two and was part of an English crew who were unbeaten on tour in 1938 during Australia's 150th anniversary celebrations. Phyllis was also a gifted writer who recorded her memories of her father in both prose and poetry. First, here are extracts from an article she wrote in 1971, the centenary of his birth:

ON THE FAMILY STRUGGLES

"With the death of his father, Joshua, the family's fortunes deteriorated even more, and it was this grinding poverty together with the courageous struggles of his mother to survive and bring up her children decently that left my father with what he once described to me as 'iron in my soul'. He never forgot his early poverty and this manifested itself in a certain remoteness of spirit at various times, a withdrawing into himself when the memory of his childhood became too poignant in contrast with that of his own children, so happy and well provided for that we were."

ON TIME-KEEPING

"JH was a stickler for punctuality with a very pronounced capital P. 'Time is time', he would say, 'and if you are expected to be at a certain place at a certain time, it is your duty to be there, come what may'. He never deviated from this principle but would set off for any appointment long before it was necessary, simply to ensure being there 'on the dot'. Each morning he would arise at 7.45am precisely and arrive at the breakfast table freshly shaven and meticulously groomed at exactly 8.15. No slovenliness was ever permitted and his rigid self-discipline never relaxed."

ON THE IMPORTANCE OF ROUTINE

"Routine was not just an idea but a way of life, and throughout his 91 years he kept to an inflexible schedule. Meals were eaten at the same time every day, certain papers read at certain times, his various duties carried out at the appointed moment in the 24 hours. This, of course, had to be adjusted when he was away competing in tournaments, but even then he kept as close to his routine as possible. His nature was such that a well-ordered and disciplined life was the only way to live as far as he was concerned - anything unorthodox, unconventional or haphazard was anathema to him and he would have none of it."

ON TAKING IT EASY

"For relaxation, reading took precedence over everything else. . . the daily papers were as necessary to him as the air he breathed, no fewer than five being delivered, this, of course, included evening editions. JH had a fetish about papers, they had to be kept scrupulously in order and woe betide the person who left one crumpled and the pages in disarray. 'A paper has a soul,' he would thunder, glowering at the offender from beneath frowning brow as he carefully smoothed the pages and put them in the right sequence. Indeed, in his latter years, mother had to tack down the middle pages of *The Times* each day with needle and thread to ensure orderliness, a chore which sometimes elicited from her a pointed remark on the absurdity of people's fads."

ON BEING A FATHER

"He was strict and a disciplinarian, but with seven lively, rampageous children he had to be. He was also loving and just, inordinately generous and deeply protective - the welfare of his wife and children were all that mattered to him and he devoted his life to that end. His integrity and greatness of character shone through all he said and did, the same gracious courtesy was shown to the most humble as to those of greater eminence. Modesty and humility he had in abundance despite the worldwide fame that was his, and although he did indeed mix with kings and princes he never lost the common touch, most eloquent proof of his stature as a great man."

PHYLLIS shared this amusing anecdote with the gathering at St Margaret's Church, Northam, for the re-dedication of three stained glass windows in JH's memory in 1997:

"During the First World War he joined the local Volunteer Force, the pre-runners, I suppose, of Dad's Army. They were not in uniform but wore a scarlet armband with "GR" in gold lettering. Sunday morning they marched, rifles on shoulders, from the Drill Hall in Park Street to Richmond Park, about a mile-and-a-half away. Soon after 10.30am we would hear the tramp of hob-nailed boots and out we would rush to see him pass by. Quite against King's Regulations, I'm sure, he would wave to us as he went."

SHE also composed the following hymn, adapted to the tune of Melita (For Those in Peril on the Sea), which was sung at the same re-dedication service, and a poem about her father which she called The Old Timer. An amended version of the poem was read at the service:

Maker of all whose mighty hand
Created sea and sky and land
And in the corner of the West
RND's links, one's skills to test
At playing golf this ancient game
When life is never quite the same!

No rain or wind or weather joke
Can damp the zeal of golfing folk
With clubs on trolley studded shoes
They set forth as on a pleasure cruise
And as they place their ball on tee
May they receive some help from Thee

As far ahead as trouble stare
They see the bunkers everywhere
Some to the right and others left
To feel of any hope bereft
Oh help them pitch up to the pin
And see that white ball drop right in

A happy band these golfers are
Who talk of birdies, making par
Of hooks and slices, stance and swing
And chipping, putting, pivoting.
All you who play this ancient game
Just thank the Lord and praise His name

THE OLD TIMER

John Henry was a Devon man, a fine and worthy breed,
A champion of golfers, he, it must be agreed,
Upon the links at Westward Ho! he learnt to play the game
Then as a fair-haired boy set forth to win renown and fame.

He played in turn the leading ones, both amateur and pro
This unknown golfer from the West drubbed all and laid them low,
And then across the Border he challenged Scottish might,
For until then no English pro had put their pride to flight.

John Henry he had wrists of steel, with forearms strong as iron,
Strength in his shoulders, thighs and legs - the courage of a lion,
So JH took on "Andra" and won by four and three,
First Englishman to beat a Scot in all their history.

Five British Open Championships he won against the best,
And six times he was second, a record none contest,
The German and the French he won, the latter two years running,
As match-play champion more than once, his victories were stunning.

And when the rain lashed down non-stop, the wind in vicious squall,
With cap pulled down and jutting jaw, rocklike he played the ball
Straight as an arrow through the gale, impervious it flew
As JH, with triumphant grunt, sublimely followed through.

His mastery of every shot, consistent through the years,
The crisp, clean swing, faultless approach, control of nerves and fears,
The chip shot with his mashie but inches from the pin,
The crouching stance, the deft, sure touch to sink the putt well in.

This was the Maestro of the links, a sportsman to the core,
Who raised the status of the pro to where it is, and more,
Respected, loved, acclaimed by all, whatever their estate,
John Henry Taylor, humbly born, became JH the Great.

HAROLD BEGBIE, the journalist, author and poet, became great friends with JH Taylor. Begbie, a keen golf enthusiast, invited his pal down to the New Forest for a few days' golf during which Taylor not only passed on some invaluable tuition tips but also shared his passionate views on a wide variety of current issues facing the nation. Here, in the book that he based on the trip, *JH TAYLOR or The Inside of a Week*, Begbie paints a striking verbal portrait of the great man. Sadly, Begbie died just four years after the book was published by Mills and Boon in 1925:

ALTHOUGH he is the average height of the present generation and carries himself with an almost rigid uprightness, Taylor, by reason of his immense breadth, passes for a small man. He carries on shoulders that would do honour to a Guardsman a head that Caesar might have envied - huge, nobly-shaped, and dense in bone. The forehead overhangs the face, the complexion of which is pale, and the small eyes, grey-blue in colour, are of a singular intensity.

The delicate nose is small and aquiline, something too ladylike for so masculine a face, but the chin amply atones for this concession to tenderness: by an aggression as formidable as a puncher's fist.

It is the face of a fighter. It advertises a dogmatic spirit, a tenacious mind, and a warrior heart. No wonder that Sir Richard Grenville is his favourite Englishman and that he rejoices in the great sea exploits of his Devonshire countrymen.

Someone has admirably described him in a Championship as streaming ahead of the crowd like forked lightning and conveying the sense that thunderbolts are under his jurisdiction. It would seem that on such occasions his stocky and thickset body is impelled by a spirit that is for ever chafing to mount up like an eagle, and that his heart is occupied only by a titanic desire to get at somebody and flay him alive.

There is indeed a murderous power about the man when he is really fighting for a victory, and it is a curious thing to observe how this murderous instinct manifests itself in his face.

The eyes narrow to almost invisible slits, the little nose becomes the beak of a peregrine, the mouth assumes a merciless compression, and the aggressive chin presses forward like the bows of an

WAR AND PEACE: On the course John Henry fought with the heart of a warrior; off it, according to his friend, Harold Begbie, he displayed a smile of the friendliest geniality

ironclad. Every movement of the body is quick and decisive, as if he had never lounged in his life or hesitated for an instant between any yea or any nay.

Yet this picture presents only a fighting mood. It is entirely misleading as to the fundamentals of his disposition. In repose, the almost invisible slits become the kindest and most affectionate of eyes; the grim mouth loosens to a smile of the friendliest geniality; the great chin relaxes till it is as humorous as the chin of Fielding; and the broad brow, instead of being black with thunder, is sunny with good nature.

In other words, JH Taylor is a Christian "whose face is a love-letter to all mankind", until he sets out to trample into the dust one particular member of the human race.

JH TAYLOR'S rise to fame made him an A-list celebrity in the eyes of the good and the great who were fast discovering the attractions of golf.

It would, of course, be an exaggeration to insist that no event of any credible social standing was complete without the presence of the Open champion, but clearly Taylor's diary was brimming with offers from both at home and abroad.

The boy from the backwaters of rural North Devon truly did mix with monarchs. No-one realised quite how far it would lead at the time, but Taylor's introduction to celebrity began early.

While a caddie at Royal North Devon in 1884, he was assigned the bag of Prince Windisch-Gratz, who would later become prime minister of Austria.

The prince came to Britain to escape a cholera scare on the Continent and while visiting Westward Ho! decided to try his hand at golf.

Taylor wrote in a magazine interview: "I was deputed to attend to His Highness's wants. He was a hopeless beginner, but I tolerated this, thinking myself compensated by the dignity that the employment conferred."

Taylor, being the pragmatic gentleman that he was, no doubt "tolerated" many more of the Establishment figures he would encounter over the years, often at "Country House" parties where leading professionals of the day were hired on lucrative contracts to teach golf to the family and friends of wealthy landowners.

But through their affinity with golf, he also forged many friendships - some long and strong, others more fleeting - with characters from all walks of life. Taylor's People were an eclectic crew, and here are just a few of them:

BERNARD DARWIN

THE golf writer and author saw at first hand Taylor's ascent to golfing greatness and they became life-long friends. Taylor said: "About my game he has often written that I not only have to fight it, but myself as well. The truth of this I candidly admit, for I believe Mr Darwin is similarly afflicted. It is evidence of the greatness of the game that a philosopher and sage who can write with such urbanity and charm on its varied aspects can be as human as the rest of us when put to the test. It is not too much to say that his essays and articles are regularly read by thousands who have never handled a club."

SIR ERNEST SHACKLETON

A BRIEF encounter while at Dornoch, in Scotland, but one long enough for Taylor to make this sound assessment of the Antarctic explorer: "I don't think he played golf, but I still have a vivid recollection of his manly appearance, his grave face lit by a pair of steely blue eyes which to me were indicative of the indomitable courage that his subsequent achievements proved was not illusory."

SIR HARRY LAUDER

TAYLOR first met the world-famous entertainer during a golfing tour of Scotland and Lauder, yet to be knighted, invited him to stay at his house at Dunoon and play a few rounds with him. JH wrote: "Nothing could have exceeded the kindness and hospitality shown

FUNNY GAME: Entertainer Sir Harry Lauder, teeing off here at Royal Mid-Surrey, would have his playing partners in fits during a round. PICTURE COURTESY OF ROYAL MID-SURREY GOLF CLUB

to me by Mr and Mrs Lauder. As one would expect, he was as amusing on the course as he was on the stage, which made any serious effort at concentration difficult to attempt.

"One night, Mr Lauder was showing me his many treasures gathered during his world travels when he exclaimed suddenly: 'Come awa in tae the ither room and I'll show you the greatest treasure in the hoose ...Yon's the stool I sat on as a wee laddie to sup my porridge afore I went doon the pit at half-past five in the mornin' and I widna pairt wi' it for all the siller in the world.' I wish I were capable of putting into these simple statements the intensity of feeling that Mr Lauder put into them."

JH doesn't say so, but perhaps it was also a chilling reminder of the starkness of his own upbringing.

HIS IMPERIAL HIGHNESS, THE GRAND DUKE MICHAEL OF RUSSIA

TO SOME this may come as a surprise, but the Russian nobleman was a founder and president of the Cannes golf club, and Taylor first came across him while playing in a tournament involving British and French professionals. They were swish surroundings, but apparently the clubhouse was not a place to dine if you were suddenly struck with hunger. His Highness and entourage took lunch there every day, but no-one was allowed to take their seats until they arrived!

That said, Taylor remembers him as "kindly and usually most considerate" and someone with a "patent and sincere" love for the game. "It should be remembered, too," said Taylor, "that he proved to be a loyal friend of this country at its time of great tribulation."

THE AGA KHAN

TAYLOR'S enduring friendship with The Aga Khan blossomed out of the blue. He wrote: "One morning in the spring of 1919 I was in my shop at Mid-Surrey when in walked a stoutish-built, swarthy gentleman of Asiatic origin who, to my surprise, introduced himself as The Aga Khan. I had been recommended to him by an old friend as an instructor likely to improve his golf.

"As was but natural, I was very willing to take on the job in the hope of extending the acquaintance, with an eye to future emoluments. He proved a most apt pupil, and I hope I was able to improve his game. His assiduity and anxiety to learn certainly deserved it. At 8.30 every morning he was driven down to Mid-Surrey, fresh-looking, alert and vigorous. He would have an hour's intense practice and, just as promptly, would hurry back to London content, I hope, with the day well begun."

The friendship developed and JH was invited on a month's golfing holiday, which he readily accepted. They met at The Ritz, in Paris, where Taylor found that a suite of rooms had been reserved for him, and played golf at St Cloud. His friend insisted on a wager of 25 francs a round. "I gave him 16 shots," said Taylor. "Occasionally, I lost and it was a source of quiet delight for me to notice how gleefully the meagre winnings were pocketed."

They moved on to Switzerland, staying at the most exclusive hotels and playing the finest courses before returning to France. "We travelled back to Paris where I was paid off and thus ended one of the most delightful holidays in the companionship of one of the kindest, most warm-hearted and lavishly-generous gentlemen I have ever been privileged to meet."

• *The Aga Khan is the hereditary title of the Imam - or leader - of the Nizari Muslims, the largest branch of the Isma'ili followers of the Shi'a faith.*

EMPEROR HIROHITO OF JAPAN

AS CROWN PRINCE, the future Emperor travelled to Europe in 1921 and was such a regular visitor to Mid-Surrey that JH had a personalised set of clubs made up for him at his factory in Sheen. Imagine, then, the patriotic Taylor's emotions when his young pupil, now Emperor, sanctioned the attack on Pearl Harbour which brought both Japan and the United States into the Second World War.

CHARLES "KID" McCOY

TAYLOR was on deck travelling back from the United States when he "fell into conversation with a young man, smartly dressed, with athleticism recorded in every movement, who introduced himself as Kid McCoy and informed me he was making the trip eastwards in search of engagements and fresh glories within the roped-off square."

With McCoy was his manager, Mr Kelly, "a melancholy-looking gentleman with but one arm" who was also known as The Parson.

Taylor said: "I found McCoy a very likeable fellow and we struck up a minor and brief friendship. His itinerary demanded that he left the boat at Charlestown and he invited me to tour Ireland with him in some sort of capacity as an additional attraction to his drawing powers. What my part was to be I never understood and I had no hesitation in turning the offer down."

It was a good call. Fact blurs with fiction in the colourful life of Kid McCoy. He had invented the lethal "corkscrew" punch after watching a cat attacking a cotton ball on a string and became world middleweight champion in 1897. But he didn't defend his title, instead moving up to light-heavyweight where he had an impressive, if controversial, career without ever landing another world crown. In 1924, McCoy, reputedly married ten times, three of those to the same woman, was jailed for the manslaughter of his wealthy lover. He always protested his innocence, claiming she had shot herself.

JIMMY WILDE

CLEARLY, Taylor had a fascination for boxing, and he was in awe of the courage and skills of the Welsh world flyweight champion. He met Wilde - 130 wins, just four defeats and 15 draws in 149 fights - when Wilde and his pal, the heavyweight "Bombardier" Billy Wells, turned to golf as a form of relaxation.

Taylor wrote: "Jimmy will forgive me when I say that his efforts at playing golf do not begin to compare with the devastation he wrought among his opponents, whereas Billy's form at golf approximated to that of a scratch player.

"As my interest in boxing increased, so did my admiration for those champions and I lost few opportunities of seeing my favourites in action. Like the rest of the world, I was continually amazed at Jimmy's pulverising and destructive power. He well

LORD OF THE RING:
Welshman Jimmy Wilde
suffered only four defeats
in 149 fights

deserved the name of 'Tylorstown Terror', but when I knew him better I held it to be a grave misnomer, for anything less than Jimmy's normal appearance and demeanour, charming smile and soft Welsh accent was difficult to conceive."

WG GRACE

JH met the legend of English cricket through a mutual friend, George Beldam, the Middlesex opener, and the trio played together at Mid-Surrey.

Taylor said: "It was a delightful experience for me, made more lasting when I saw how The Doctor enjoyed the game with all the zest of a small boy. 'Boyish' is the right word to use, no other can adequately describe the real fun that he got from it. He had a style of his own, a short, sharp backswing with plenty of wrist action. He drove the ball a long distance and was a deadly holer-out, using a diminutive aluminium putter that looked like a toy in his big hands and huge frame. My brief acquaintanceship with Dr Grace broadened into the reverent respect that everyone who had known or met him had for his delightful and cheery personality."

LORD DE GREY, LATER MARQUIS OF RIPON

TAYLOR had been invited to a Country House golf party, where he witnessed the skills of a politician who most certainly would not have made the Christmas card list of the Royal Society for the Protection of Birds. Taylor wrote: "Lord de Grey was world renowned as a shot and it fascinated me to see the deadly way he dealt with every unfortunate bird that came within range of his gun." But perhaps the man standing next in line with de Grey was more interesting. JH remembers Mr Winston Churchill as "a tall, lanky youth who had not long returned from his exciting adventures in the Boer War". Churchill was shooting, "with indifferent success", but he was already unleashing the oratory that would later captivate the world.

THE DUKE, THE KING AND THE PRIME MINISTER

IT'S OFF to Chatsworth House for one of the highlights of the social calendar - and this year the hosts, the Duke and Duchess of Devonshire, have been honoured by the presence of His Majesty King Edward Vll and Queen Alexandra.

Taylor, along with Scottish professional Ben Sayers, was providing the expert advice. Taylor recalled: "The Duke was almost childlike with delight when he succeeded, which was seldom, in lifting the ball into the air and pushing it a few yards.

"The King did not play, but contented himself by riding on the back of a stout pony to watch the efforts of other guests and passing jocular remarks about their inability to rise above mediocrity."

Everything was going well until one afternoon when Taylor found himself partnering Lord Stanley, later Earl of Derby, in an England v Scotland foursomes with Sayers and Arthur Balfour, the British prime minister from 1902-1905.

Somehow, at the 17th hole, Sayers' drive became lodged up a tree. It was Balfour's shot next and under the Rules of Golf, in the absence of any local ruling, the ball should either be played "as it

A LAW UNTO HIMSELF: Prime Minister Balfour didn't like the ruling when his partner's ball landed in a tree, so he sat down and re-wrote the regulations for all future Chatsworth golf events.

lies" - that is, from up in the tree - or the hole conceded. Balfour would have none of it, claiming that "under the laws of equity I should be allowed to drop another ball without penalty." When that wasn't accepted, he marched on to the next hole.

Taylor continued: "The following morning I was told that directly after dinner the previous evening, where the incident was the main topic of conversation and debate, Balfour retired to his room early and at breakfast produced a set of rules dealing with all and every contingency, including the one responsible. As far as I know they were adopted as the definitive rules governing play on the Chatsworth course!"

Taylor's festival ended in grand but bizarre fashion. Keen to return to London as quickly as possible, Taylor was smuggled aboard the Royal Train by his friend, Jack Hawkins, the king's personal attendant, on the strict understanding that he was to keep out of sight at all costs. He wrote: "Thus I rode, if not in triumph, certainly with expedition to St Pancras."

THE FAMILY TAYLOR, 1913: JH and his wife Clara with their children, back row, Margery, Dorothy and Jack, and, front row, Lesley, Audrey, Phyllis and Cicely

RUGBY REVELLER: Golf was his life's work, but boxing and the oval ball game were two of JH's passions. He was an energetic wing-forward for Northam Colts (pictured here in the back row, fourth from the right in 1890) and loved to go to Twickenham for England games, particularly the Calcutta Cup matches against "the old enemy" Scotland.

PAUSE FOR THOUGHT: JH takes time out to relax but he wasn't usually one to sit on the fence!

THIRD-CLASS CITIZENS?

9

THE Open "Special" rolled across the border into Scotland for the 1895 Championship at St Andrews. As at Sandwich the year before, the organising committee had negotiated a discounted train fare to persuade players to make the long journey north.

It was a good deal - for some. The reduced return ticket was only marginally more than the normal single fare - but it was first class for the amateurs and third class for the professionals.

There would be no exceptions - not even for the defending champion, John Henry Taylor.

He wrote of their treatment in that era: "These were the bad old days - thank goodness long since passed - when the professional was regarded as something of a nuisance and his presence as being something akin to an intrusion.

"Certainly he was tolerated - at Championship times - as a necessary sort of evil, and this impression was heightened by the fact that scarcely any provision was extended to him in the way of accommodation and simple creature comforts. He had to fend for himself the best he could.

"The clubhouse was rigorously denied him, with the result that only a wooden shed was allowed in which he could change his clothes and stow his clubs, if willing to take this not inconsiderable risk. The more cautious, of which I was one, had no alternative than to lug our clubs along to our diggings and cart them back the following morning.

"We also received a solemn censure forbidding letters being addressed to the club under pain, if not of actual confiscation, of

PRO PROTEST: Barred from the locker room, American Walter Hagen hired a car and changed in full view of the club house.

threats of non-delivery, which I thought to be unnecessarily unjust. This is not a grumble. The pro had to accept the conditions as part of the order of things, but as these reminiscences are true of the times of which I write, I feel it is a duty to record them."

Despite representations from the Professional Golfers' Association, it was a problem that wasn't to go away quickly. In 1920 at Deal, the pros again had to change in the professional's shop and the American, Walter Hagen, famously hired a car in which he "disrobed" in full view of the clubhouse - Henry Cotton would later make a similar protest by lunching on his Fortnum and Mason hamper in a car park.

In 1922, there were complaints about overcharging by caddies and insufficient toilet facilities for players, and in 1927 the PGA was forced to hire a room in the Grand Hotel at St Andrews because there were still no acceptable facilities for its members.

THIS ATTITUDE towards the golf professional was not confined to the Royal and Ancient club - it mirrored the culture that permeated the whole game in the early years. It is a simple and stark reminder that, in that era, the club pro was very much the servant of his master.

The PGA's Centenary book puts it bluntly: "For some professionals, golf brought economic prosperity, for none of them did it bring social equality."

For a rare talent like Taylor, the clubs were prepared to trade a slightly more relaxed regime for the kudos of having an Open champion on their books.

But for the average professional, the clubs called all the shots when they "negotiated" with their prospective employee.

Peter N Lewis, Director of Film Archive at The R&A and a prolific writer on golf, including the superb *Dawn of Professional Golf*, informs us that the basic "retainer" for a professional was rarely more than 20 shillings (£1) a week and the stipulated hours were long - often from 7.30am or eight o' clock until "the last player left the course."

The club professional, to varying degrees, might be expected to provide club-making and repair facilities, golf tuition, the supervision of caddies and some level of course management as well as running his shop.

Yet clubs would regularly dictate what he could charge for teaching - typically, 3s6d (17.5p) for a round or 2s (10p) for an hour's tuition - and, well into the 20th Century, they might set the price for club repairs and equipment, with the professional perhaps earning between £70 and £150 a year.

Often, the club would insist that its pro must not leave the course without permission and was allowed into the clubhouse only on the rare occasions when he was invited.

It was a tough life, and some were forced to revert to their old trades during the winter months to balance the books.

It wasn't much better for those with the talent and ambition to try their luck on the tournament scene.

Lewis records that in 1894 - the year Taylor won £30 for his first Open triumph - there was only one event other than the Championship that offered a total prize fund of more than £100.

From 1893 to 1901, the average number of tournaments each year was 13 with average total prize money of £55, though by 1914 this would rise to 31 tournaments with almost £91 in the prize pot.

Taylor topped £100 a year in gross tournament earnings only four times before the First World War, so it was no surprise that club professionals sought other avenues to augment their earnings.

They came initially in the shape of challenge matches, often arranged by clubs or individual members so they could bet on the outcome - the winning professional would receive a percentage of the stake. Later, the emphasis switched to exhibition matches set up by the players themselves or their sponsors.

Taylor's first real taste of the challenge format was his victory over Andrew Kirkaldy in the Burnham-Winchester showdown in 1892 and, as with all the leading players, it was a vital source of income.

Lewis's research reveals that between 1894 and 1914, Taylor clocked up 529 matches, at an average of just over 25 a year and peaking at 45 in 1910. Harry Vardon, despite bouts of ill health, topped that with 544 at an average of 27 each year, and James Braid totted up an amazing 54 matches in 1910 on his way to a total of 526.

With an average first prize of just over £14 and marginally under £8 for second place, Lewis estimates that, after expenses, their coffers would have been swelled by around £7 a match.

Of course, being an Open champion dramatically raised the bar in terms of new financial opportunities.

With a higher profile after his first win at Sandwich in 1894, Taylor was able to attract higher fees - and more of them.

Almost sheepishly, he recalls that he twice lost £50 stakes put up by one sponsor, the publisher Sir George Newnes - against Kirkaldy in 1895 and Willie Park a year later - but it is safe to assume that over the course of their "partnership" Newnes finished comfortably on the right side of the bottom line.

By 1905, the stakes had risen even higher. Newspaper proprietors Edward Hulton and George Riddell each put up £200 for a marathon England v Scotland foursomes match.

Taylor and Vardon, backed by Hulton, took on Riddell's pairing of Braid and Sandy Herd in a 144-hole contest - 36 holes each over

St Andrews, Royal Troon, Royal Lytham and St Annes and Royal Cinque Ports at Deal. The match certainly captured the public's imagination because around 10,000 fans turned up to watch the opening salvos at St Andrews - and it was the home crowd who were cheering after the first day as their men led by two holes.

But their joy was short-lived. By the end of the second leg at Troon the following week, the English were 12 up and they finally closed out the match after 132 holes, winning 13 and 12 on a foul day at Deal.

It was Riddell who had to hand over the money.

IF THE first steps of JH Taylor's journey to golfing greatness were almost certainly taken by pony-and-trap, then it was the train that kept his career on track.

JH and his peers were probably more familiar with railway timetables than they were with the Rules of Golf as they plotted their way to and from the tournaments and exhibition matches that formed a substantial part of their earning power.

Taylor had no inclination to learn to drive and, anyway, even by 1910 only 14,000 cars and commercial vehicles were built that year in the United Kingdom.

So it was the train that took the strain, a network of private companies providing a far more comprehensive service than the post-Beeching era of today. For golf professionals like Taylor, the train was crucial to their livelihoods.

Even the 500-mile trek from Winchester to Prestwick for his Open Championship debut in 1893 wasn't as daunting as it might seem.

North Devon railway enthusiast Lewis Andrews says: "Winchester Station was opened by the London and South Western Railway in 1839 and by 1893 there was a direct service to London Waterloo.

"Taylor might have got off at Clapham Junction or continued to Waterloo before using the basic underground system that existed in London at that time to make his way across the capital to Euston. There he could have caught a train to Glasgow Central, changing for Prestwick Town Station - which is still open."

The journey takes just over six hours today: in the late 1890s the Special Scotch Express - the service wasn't then officially known as the Flying Scotsman - was running between London and Edinburgh in eight-and-a-half hours.

Finding suitable connecting trains for all his travels - particularly at night - was a problem, though, and it was one of the factors that drove Taylor's desire to base himself in London.

OPEN GOLD

10

JOHN HENRY TAYLOR was a titan of golf whose exploits helped to propel his sport into the heart of the public consciousness. He was a true British superstar.

His epic Open Championship battles with fellow Englishman Harry Vardon and Scotland's James Braid captured the imagination of a sporting nation in a way that the game had never managed before.

In 1914, with all three players locked on five Open victories, Vardon beat Taylor in a dramatic "shoot-out" at Prestwick to clinch an historic sixth title - a record that remains to this day - but Taylor's was still a stellar career.

A byword for accuracy and consistency, at 5ft8in Taylor wasn't a tall man, but he had huge shoulders and massively powerful forearms. These attributes, allied to hours spent on the wind- or rain-swept links at Royal North Devon, helped him to acquire a reputation as the best bad-weather golfer of his generation.

Largely self-taught, he confided in his autobiography: "From the first I found the game was easy. Watching carefully (as a caddie) the better players, I tried to embody in my attempts to play the game the better points of each, but later discovered that I had evolved a style entirely my own. My rather cramped and rigid swing I attribute to my desire to cheat the wind which blows with varying intensity most days at Westward Ho!"

Developing the theme in *Golf Monthly* in 1950, Taylor wrote: "A player should consider his golfing education incomplete if he cannot overcome the malicious nature of the wind. To play golf decently well in favourable weather conditions is a comparatively

TAYLOR'S GOLD: Now part of The R&A collection in the British Golf Museum at St Andrews, these are the five Gold Medals that JH Taylor won for his Open triumphs.

The first winner's medal was presented in 1872, when no trophy was available. Early versions of the Gold Medal, which in fact were silver gilt, were large ovals with a central design of a shield and crossed clubs. Around the edge was the inscription "Golf Champion Trophy". During the late 1880s and early 1890s, the design of the medal changed several times and the current circular medal was introduced in 1893. The basic size and shape has not changed since then.

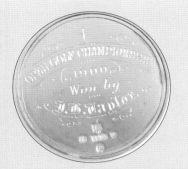

That same year, the medal was given a value of £10 and this was deducted from the advertised purse for the winner of the Open. So when JH Taylor won his first Championship, at Sandwich in 1894, his "official" prize money was £40, but he only received £30, plus, of course, the medal. In 1920, the value of the winner's medal was increased to £25 and again deducted from his share of the prize fund. This practice stopped after the 1929 Open Championship and from 1930 onwards, the winner no longer had to "pay" for his medal.

The R&A bought the medals in 1981 for a fee believed to be £13,000

PICTURES BY KIND PERMISSION OF THE ROYAL AND ANCIENT GOLF CLUB OF ST ANDREWS

easy matter. To play well when the wind is in a devilish mood is a much more difficult proposition.

"It was perhaps a precocious thought I claimed as my own that to conquer the wind a different way of stance and swing was necessary. Trial soon proved that the tall, dashing, flowing swing shown by Horace Hutchinson, my early hero, was of little use in controlling the ball.

"Experiment taught me that a compact swing was the answer with the right arm close to the side, a restricted hip pivot and a short follow-through with the ball more opposite the right than the left foot, enabling it to be struck as the clubhead descends toward the downward arc of the swing.

"This apparent cramped style has not the appeal which attends, as may be its due, the flowing follow-through so artistically enhanced in a photograph but, beautiful as the sight is, it is the actual result that counts."

It was a tried and tested method that brought him handsome rewards.

IN THE SWING: JH shows the form that made him a golfing great with five Open wins

In all, Taylor competed in 31 Opens during a 36-year Championship marathon - his first at Prestwick in 1893 and his swansong at Muirfield in 1929.

He won the Claret Jug in 1894, 1895, 1900, 1909 and 1913 - and just missed out on a hat-trick of victories in 1896 when he lost an 18-hole play-off to Vardon. It was one of six second-place finishes in the Open, with four of those coming in consecutive years from 1904. The last was in 1914.

His victory at Sandwich in 1894 was the first by an English professional - John Ball, in 1890, and Harold Hilton (1892) had won as amateurs - and the time-span of 19 years between his first and last Open triumphs remains a record.

In 1924, at the age of 53, he climbed to fifth place on the final leader board, a 16th top-five finish matched only by the American legend Jack Nicklaus. Had the two qualifying rounds been taken into the equation, Taylor would have won the Championship.

In a career that was pure gold for golfing statisticians, JH is one of only three players to win in three decades - 1894, 1900 and 1913 - along with Vardon (1896, 1903 and 1911) and the South African Gary Player (1959, 1968 and 1974).

He is also one of only four players to win an Open wire-to-wire - he achieved the feat in 1900, Vardon did it in 1899 and 1903, with the American "Supermex" Lee Trevino (1971) and Player (1974) completing the quartet.

In 1904, Taylor's last-round 68 - one of three sub-70 scores that year - was an all-time Championship low. He thrilled the crowd as he chased a 67 that would have tied him with the winner Jack White - and he would have made it had his putt on the last green not lipped out of the hole. "It was," he would say later, "the most exciting tournament I ever played in."

Ironically, his Championship-low record came on the same Sandwich links where he had won ten years earlier with the highest-ever winning aggregate total (326).

In 1900, he finished runner-up to Vardon in the US Open, but could manage only tied 30th when he returned to America in 1913.

Stung by Frenchman Arnaud Massy's Open victory the previous year, Taylor went to La Boulie, near Versailles, in 1908 and exacted revenge for Britain's professional golfers by taking the French

HERE'S what was happening in the world in 1894 when JH won his first Open Championship at Sandwich:

• THE REBIRTH of the Olympic Games was still two years away
• QUEEN VICTORIA was 57 years into her 64-year reign and her Prime Ministers were William Gladstone and the Earl of Rosebery. Gladstone had resigned over high Naval estimates. The 24th President of the United States was Grover Cleveland
• LOCAL Government Act created parish councils and gave women the vote in local elections
• NOTTS COUNTY won the FA Cup, beating Bolton Wanderers at Goodison Park to become the first club outside the top division to win the trophy
• MANCHESTER Ship Canal opened
• MARKS and Spencer started life as a market stall in Leeds
• LADAS, owned by the Earl of Rosebery, won the Derby at odds of 2-9, the shortest priced winner in the race's history. Why Not, ridden by Arthur Nightingall, won the Grand National
• TOWER Bridge, in London, opened to traffic. Blackpool Tower opened
• FRENCH anarchist Martial Bourdin was killed after a bomb he was carrying exploded outside the Royal Greenwich Observatory
• BORN - Harold Macmillan, Conservative Prime Minister, King Edward VIII, who abdicated so he could marry American divorcee Wallis Simpson, JB Priestley, novelist, playwright and critic, and Herbert Sutcliffe, England and Yorkshire cricketer
• DIED - Robert Louis Stevenson

national championship. He successfully defended his title the following year.

In 1912, on a Baden-Baden course that weeks of torrential rain had reduced to a "snipe bog"- Taylor's description - he added the German Open to his portfolio of victories.

He won the prestigious *News of the World* Professional Match Play title in 1904 and 1908, both at his home course of Mid-Surrey.

The *Golfers' Handbook* also records that JH represented England against Scotland on nine occasions between 1903 and 1913 - the 1908 match was washed out by the weather and the 1911 contest was played as a Coronation match between professionals and amateurs.

For someone who had survived the cauldron of so many Championship battles, Taylor made an astonishing admission long after it was all over. Writing in *Golf Monthly* in 1951, he said: "I am not ashamed to confess that I always dreaded the coming of the Championship, especially after my first win. By then I had learned what the struggle really meant, days of foreboding before the event and sleepless nights while it lasted, tribulations I tried to make myself believe the whole lot of my fellow competitors had also to suffer.

"It was difficult to persuade myself that Harry Vardon was so tortured; if he had been, he successfully hid it beneath an ever-smiling and genial countenance which nothing ever seemed to ruffle.

"In the case of Jimmy Braid, I was not quite so sure. We usually shared the same 'digs' and on a couple of occasions the same bed, so I had ample evidence that my companion in the dreary hours of wakeful darkness was not without his fear for the morrow.

"Sandy Herd also, I thought, viewed the prospect of the struggle with a deal of perturbation, trying to hide his anxiety under a cloak of levity which never misled me regarding how he felt."

At the height of his playing powers, Taylor had promised himself that when he felt he could no longer make a realistic challenge for a Championship, he would quit tournament golf.

There is some confusion about when that moment actually came. Taylor, in his autobiography, says he bowed out at Royal Lytham and St Annes in 1926 after finishing tied 11th, 13 shots behind the champion, Bobby Jones. However, official Open records reveal that he played in 1927, missed 1928 and finally called it a day at Muirfield in 1929 when, with rounds of 79 and 80, he failed to make the cut.

Taylor wrote later: "I had had a good innings, had won five Open Championships, which was enough to satisfy the reasonable ambitions of anyone, and to continue playing and torturing myself was not my idea of a graceful decline into obscurity."

The golf writer, Bernard Darwin, commented: " For many years he was the head of his profession. It is due to him, more than any other man, that the professional game has climbed so far above its old unsatisfactory condition. He is a natural speaker, a natural fighter, and a natural leader who would have made his mark in any walk of life.' Here's how JH's five Open Championship triumphs played out:

THE ROOTS for Taylor's first Open triumph had been planted a year earlier, at Prestwick.

He had gone to Ayrshire a week before that event to prepare for his first sortie into Championship golf - and immediately found himself in demand among the top Scottish professionals as a practice partner.

The conspiracy theories abounded - here, perhaps, was the chance not only to avenge the challenge match defeat of their compatriot Andrew Kirkaldy 12 months earlier but also to put a sizeable dent in the young Englishman's title aspirations.

Taylor himself noted: "I rather suspect that my defeat of Andra' had whetted their several golfing appetites, otherwise I can see no reason why they should all have wanted to have a go at me."

The ploy worked in part, but not exactly in the way they imagined.

Taylor saw off all-comers - "I took them on one by one every day for a week and emerged undefeated" - and carried that form into the Championship with a brilliant first-round 75, a then course record, to lead by three shots.

Instead of being short on self-belief, he allowed himself to become over-confident: "Like the young ass I was, the better I played the more cocksure I became and I foolishly thought the Championship was mine. It was as well that such supreme arrogance was to receive a salutary check."

In foul weather, he slumped to a second-round score of 89 that wrecked any hopes of landing the title. He would eventually finish in a tie for 10th place, 11 strokes behind the winner, Willie Auchterlonie.

Taylor left Prestwick saddened but a whole lot wiser. "I had learned a most valuable lesson, that more qualities are required to win a Championship than occasional flashes of brilliance," he wrote of his first Open appearance.

That salutary lesson still on the radar, he arrived at Sandwich, on the Kent coast, in June, 1894, and began writing his own chapter in the history of golf.

Whoever won that year was assured a special place in the record books because it was the first time that the Open had been staged outside Scotland. Taylor made it a double celebration by becoming the first English professional to lift golf's biggest prize.

Taylor wrote: "Sandwich links in 1894 had not the spit-and-polish appearance it has worn in recent years. Founded in 1887, it remained for a long time a rather desolate and windswept spot, and when first seen one could easily visualise that, as a test of golf, it was a terror."

He was disappointed with his first-round 84 - until he discovered that only one player had bettered it. He followed it with an 80 for a one-shot lead - "I slept very badly that night - the mere possibility that I might win was a nightmare" - and closed out the tournament with two rounds of 81 to beat Duggie Rolland by five strokes.

His winning aggregate total of 326 was maligned by some pundits of the day - and their comments would later invoke a rare show of anger from the new champion.

"The score has often been criticised by the unthinking as unworthy. Compared with present-day scores it appears huge, but the critics cannot have the faintest conception of what the game was at that time and the conditions under which it was played.

"It is a waste of time trying to convince them and I gave up trying long ago. But one indisputable fact should set them thinking again. At Sandwich, the best players in the world met, and if they could not return better scores it meant that existing conditions precluded lower scoring, and when that is realised there is nothing more to be said."

Taylor's view was supported by the *Golfing Annual*, which reported: "The features of Taylor's play were his wonderfully-straight driving, his extreme steadiness and, above all, his deadly approaching.

"When one compares his winning score with that of other Championships one must bear in mind the tremendous carries at Sandwich. Many a golfer must have gone home sore at heart after this acquaintance with them."

The week got even better for Taylor when he reached the final of a Gentlemen v Players competition - the first ever between amateur and professional golfers. It took his total winnings for the week to

JH TAYLOR'S OPEN RECORD

YEAR	VENUE	SCORES		POSITION
1893	Prestwick	75 - 89 - 86 - 83	333	10th
1894	Royal St George's, Sandwich	84 - 80 - 81 - 81	326	1st
1895	St Andrews	86 - 78 - 80 -78	322	1st
1896	Muirfield	77 - 78 - 81 - 80	316	2nd
1897	Royal Liverpool, Hoylake	82 - 80 - 82 - 86	330	10th =
1898	Prestwick	78 - 78 - 77 - 79	312	4th
1899	Royal St George's, Sandwich	77 - 76 - 83 - 84	320	4th
1900	St Andrews	79 - 77 - 78 - 75	309	1st
1901	Muirfield	79 - 83 - 74 - 77	313	3rd
1902	Royal Liverpool, Hoylake	81 -76 - 78 - 79	314	6th
1903	Prestwick	80 - 82 - 78 -76	316	9th
1904	Royal St George's, Sandwich	77 - 78 - 74 - 68	297	2nd =
1905	St Andrews	80 - 85 - 78 - 80	323	2nd =
1906	Muirfield	77 - 72 - 75 - 80	304	2nd
1907	Royal Liverpool, Hoylake	79 - 79 - 76 - 80	314	2nd
1908	Prestwick	79 - 77 - 76 - 75	307	7th=
1909	Royal Cinque Ports, Deal	74 - 73 - 74 - 74	295	1st
1910	St Andrews	76 - 80 - 78 - 78	312	14th=
1911	Royal St George's, Sandwich	72 - 76 - 78 - 79	305	5th=
1912	Muirfield	75 - 76- 77 - 84	312	11th=
1913	Royal Liverpool, Hoylake	73 - 75 - 77 - 79	304	1st
1914	Prestwick	74 - 78 - 74 - 83	309	2nd
1915-19	OPEN SUSPENDED DUE TO WORLD WAR ONE			
1920	Royal Cinque Ports, Deal	78 - 79 - 80 - 79	316	12th
1921	St Andrews	80 - 80 - 75 - 74	309	26th=
1922	Royal St George's, Sandwich	73 - 78 - 76 - 77	304	6th
1923	Royal Troon	80 - 78 - 79 - 79	316	44th=
1924	Royal Liverpool, Hoylake	75 - 74 - 79 - 79	307	5th
1925	Prestwick	74 - 79 - 80 - 77	310	6th=
1926	Royal Lytham and St Annes	75 - 78 - 71 - 80	304	11th=
1927	St Andrews	76 - 78 - 77 - 80	311	49th=
1928	Royal St George's, Sandwich	DID NOT PLAY		
1929	Muirfield	79 - 80 MISSED CUT		69th=

£50 - he would have had to work almost 15 months for that as a labourer - and it was a "proud and happy youngster" who made his way back to Winchester.

KEY MOMENT: His disastrous 89 at Prestwick the year before - just the wake-up call he needed.

WINNING TOTAL: 84-80-81-81 = 326. Won by five strokes.

OPEN PRIZE MONEY: £30

1895, ST ANDREWS

JH arrived for his Championship debut at the home of golf with the doomsayers full of forebodings.

There was no way, they glumly forecast, that he could defend his title at St Andrews because his favoured style of high approach shots to the greens would simply not work there.

Taylor wrote: "Those critics who knew my style of play, and many more who did not but who based their opinions on the better informed, were unanimous that my method of approaching the hole with a high-dropping cut mashie shot, while suitable to the inland, soggy greens in southern England, would prove to be most ineffective when played on to the hard, dry and skittery greens at St Andrews.

"They had forgotten that I had learned how to play this type of stroke at Westward Ho! and developed it at Burnham.

"The most eminent critic - subsequently my friend, the late Johnnie Low - went as far as to say that Taylor had no chance at St Andrews as he had never learned to play the 'run-up' shot. This appeared to me to be illogical reasoning and scarcely fair.

"True, I had never depended on the run-up as a sole means of approaching the hole - I had demonstrated to my own satisfaction that my method gave better results - but to say I had never learned it was pure nonsense. I wonder what method Mr Low thought I employed when approaching the hole at Westward Ho! in a howling gale. Not tossing the ball high into the air, surely? If I could stop the ball in Devon, I could do it in Fife."

The critics looked like they had a point when Taylor - encouraged by A J Robertson, founder and editor of *Golf* magazine, and backed with hard cash by his fellow publisher, Sir George Newnes - offered a £50-a-side challenge to any professional to play him over 36 holes at the Old Course. The challenge was accepted by Andrew Kirkaldy, the match took place on the Monday of Championship week - and Andra' gleefully made off with Sir George's money!

Taylor chose to take a positive from the match - perhaps he had got all the poor shots out of his system - but he didn't fare much better in the first round of the Championship, finishing six shots off the 80 set by Harry Vardon and already wondering if he hadn't wasted his entrance money.

His fortunes improved dramatically in round two, shooting 78 while Vardon collapsed to an 85, but that still meant he trailed the half-way leader and St Andrews specialist, Sandy Herd, by five strokes.

After round three, Taylor, with an 80, had cut the deficit to just three shots, but he would still need everything to go his way in the final round if he was successfully to defend his title.

He would get a lucky break with the weather, freshening winds and a wall of water - vintage Westward Ho! on a bad day - greeting him on the first tee.

Herd, who had started 45 minutes ahead of Taylor, struggled to cope, shooting 42 on the front nine as JH, relishing conditions that "enabled me to pitch the ball up to the foot of the pin and ram my putts home", turned in 39 to claim a share of the lead.

Taylor continued on his majestic way down the stretch and could even afford to lay up at the notorious Road Hole before claiming his second Open by four shots.

He couldn't resist a gentle jibe at his detractors when he later wrote: "It gave me a big thrill to win it on my first visit to St Andrews and an even greater satisfaction in proving that my high pitched mashie shot was as effective there as anywhere else, despite what the critics had anticipated and proclaimed with such certainty."

KEY MOMENT: When the rains came in round four.

WINNING TOTAL: 86-78-80-78 = 322. Won by four strokes.

OPEN PRIZE MONEY: £30.

JH TAYLOR had a "Greyhound" in his sights as golf entered the new century.

Harry Vardon, given the nickname by Andrew Kirkaldy, had raced to three Open titles - the first player in the modern era to do so - and Taylor was straining at the leash to emulate that feat.

His pride had no doubt been stung by an 11 and 10 defeat by Vardon in a competition in Newcastle, Co.Down, the previous year.

Taylor's Open form since his previous win at the Old Course five years earlier had been consistent - runner-up to Vardon after a play-off in 1896, then seventh and two fourths in the intervening years - but he was only knocking on the door to glory, not opening it.

As he always maintained: "Filling high-up positions, or even second place in a Championship, brings little satisfaction. It is the winning that really counts."

As in 1895, when form deserted him in his challenge match against Kirkaldy, he went into the tournament on the back of a "shockingly bad" final practice round.

But, unlike that year, this time Taylor roared out of the traps to match Vardon and his brother, Tom, shot for shot with a first-round 79. By the end of the day, by virtue of a 77 to Harry's 81, he had acquired a "comfortable, but not too reassuring" lead of four strokes at the halfway point.

If JH was in need of a calming influence around him, he found it in his playing partner for the next day.

Johnny Laidlay, twice a former Amateur champion and still one of the best-known players in Scotland, had a cheerful personality and went about his business on the course as if he enjoyed every moment of it.

Taylor wrote later: "To have the luck to partner a player comparable to Mr Laidlay is a piece of good fortune in any competition. To do so on the last day of a Championship is value for many strokes.

"To know that one's partner - not opponent - is fully alive to what is going on around him gives an invaluable encouragement. It is difficult to concentrate on the job in hand when the other fellow allows himself to degenerate into a passive onlooker intent on nothing more helpful than knocking the ball about.

"I realised my good luck when I remembered that in the 1895 Championship I was partnered by Mr Sandy Ross on the last day and, if history was to repeat itself, Mr Laidlay's partnership was a good omen."

It certainly looked that way. By the end of round three, Taylor had carded a 78 to increase his advantage over Vardon to six strokes - and what followed next was later described by JH as "one of the best rounds I ever played."

Perhaps the cushion of a six-stroke lead does relieve some of the pressure, but the job still had to be done - and he did it to near perfection.

Out in 38, back in 37, he had beaten Vardon by eight shots.

Taylor wrote: "A round of 75, even at St Andrews, is nothing much to boast about these days, but in all humility I may put forward the claim that to get to the figure in the last round of a Championship, playing with a gutty ball, is something which stirs the memory with pride."

Not just that. He had repaid a "debt" with a first Open for Mid-Surrey - and a share of history for himself.

KEY MOMENT: The company of Mr Laidlay.

WINNING TOTAL: 79-77-78-75 = 309. Won by eight strokes.

OPEN PRIZE MONEY: £50.

1909, ROYAL CINQUE PORTS, DEAL

IT HAD been nine hugely frustrating years for JH Taylor since his last win in the Open - he had finished runner-up on four consecutive occasions between 1904 and 1907 - and now both James Braid and Harry Vardon, with four triumphs apiece, were ahead of him on the Championship roll of honour.

Something had to change - and quickly - if Taylor was not to be left behind in the quest for more Open glory.

The inclusion of the Deal links on the Open rota for the first time should, perhaps, have been a portent that better days were about to return. Not only was the Royal Cinque Ports club on the Kent coast next door to Royal St George's, where Taylor had secured his first Open victory in 1894, but it also reminded him of somewhere else very close to his heart.

He wrote: "Deal was a favourite links of mine. Running along the shore of Sandwich Bay with Ramsgate in the distance to the north and the crowded shipping beyond the Downs to the south, the whole presented a picture that was pleasing and inspiring, reminding me of the flavour of my home in the West Country and of the imposing sweep of Bideford Bay and the Bristol Channel."

In other circumstances, that year's Open might well have been played at Royal North Devon. RND, along with Royal Cinque Ports had been invited to apply for Open status and reportedly was the preferred option of The Royal and Ancient Club, but in the end, largely for logistical reasons, the decision went the Deal club's way.

If the familiar surroundings seemed to have had a beneficial effect, then so did his game plan - think 74.

That was the figure he believed represented the true par for the course at that time - and he guessed that four rounds around that number, without trying to force a score, would be close to the winning total.

In fact, after a stuttering start on his opening nine holes of the tournament - he went out in 41 - he would shoot one under his target for the Championship to win by six strokes from Scotland's Braid and the Englishman, Tom Ball.

Bernard Darwin, the golf writer and author, waxed lyrical about Taylor's performance, which, of course, took him level with his two closest adversaries on four Opens each.

He wrote: "It always seems to me that the most memorable Championships I have watched have been those which Taylor won. Yet Taylor, when he wins, nearly always wins easily. He takes on one of his irresistible moods and leaves his field like a streak of lightning.

"Taylor often begins with a little misfortune and emerges like a man transfigured. It was thus in the Championship at Deal. Everything seemed to be going wrong for him by inches in the first nine holes and he was making heavy weather of it.

"With the turn of the round came the turn of the tide. Taylor holed a putt for a three at the 10th and there was no holding him.

He came home like a roaring lion, and for the next three rounds he played with his most unvarying and brilliant accuracy. It was clear that there could not possibly be another champion. There was nobody else to watch."

KEY MOMENT: Sticking to the plan.

WINNING TOTAL: 74-73-74-74 = 295. Won by six strokes.

OPEN PRIZE MONEY: £50.

1913, ROYAL LIVERPOOL, HOYLAKE

THE GREEN is shiny and bare as the ball arcs slowly on its five-foot journey towards the hole, catches the right-hand side of the cup and teeters agonisingly around the edge. . .

Drop, and the dream is still alive; lip out, and the chance of a record-equalling fifth Open title is over before it began. Perhaps, at the age of 42, over for ever.

The Open field had been split into three qualifying groups, with the top 20 and ties from each section going through to the Championship proper.

Standing on the 36th hole, Taylor had received "one of the biggest frights of my life" to discover that he needed a five at the final hole merely to take his place in the main event.

"The last hole at Hoylake is not a difficult hole," he wrote later, "a driver and a pitch over the cross bunker on to the green. Most probably it was nerves, but whatever happened I failed to get properly hold of the ball with my pitch shot and into the bunker it went.

"I dug it out into some rough stuff at the back of the green and scuffled it to within a couple of yards of the hole. I can see that putt now and the word 'relief' is not sufficiently intense in its meaning to describe how I felt when the ball disappeared, dropping in with a sickening wobble on the right-hand side, a sure indication that the ball was not struck with firmness and conviction."

But the scare was over, he had made it with one stroke to spare - and he was not about to squander his good fortune this time.

Hoylake had not been particularly kind to him on his three previous Open visits, which was a disappointment because he had looked on it fondly in the early days as a "second home" to Royal North Devon.

Finishing runner-up to the Frenchman, Arnaud Massy, in 1907 merely "engrained the belief that Hoylake was not a course that suited my style".

What unfolded over the two days of this tournament was to change that perception.

Tied for the lead with the defending champion, Ted Ray, on 73 after the first round, and just one behind at the halfway stage with Vardon and Braid languishing down the field, Taylor took to his bed that night in relatively confident mood.

But neither he nor any of his rivals could have anticipated the appalling change in the weather conditions that greeted them on the next morning.

Taylor, a veteran of Westward Ho! winters, wrote: "I know something of what a gale of wind is like, but this visitation was much worse than I ever experienced. It was a full-throated hurricane, the wind blowing in intermittent gusts that were overwhelming and accompanied with sheets of torrential rain.

"I was timed to start at 9.25 and the sight of the large marquees and smaller tents flattened to the ground was depressing enough to crush every optimistic desire and outlook."

So if his final round at St Andrews in 1900 had been "one of his finest ever", then his third-round 77 here was the best of his career.

His description of the long third perhaps personifies his performance: "It was slap into the eye of the gale. It took me three full clouts and I still found myself 60 yards short, but laying a low, running iron to within a couple of yards and holing the putt I got what must have been the best five I ever obtained."

Ray had clung on gamely with an 81, but Taylor led by three and a final round of 79, played thankfully in less demanding conditions, clinched victory by the handsome margin of eight strokes.

Hoylake was to be the last of his five Open triumphs - and only his first win at Sandwich 19 years earlier ranked higher in his personal list of golfing achievements.

KEY MOMENTS: That five-footer in qualifying and the 77 in round three - the round of his life.

WINNING TOTAL: 73-75-77-79 = 304. Won by eight strokes.

OPEN PRIZE MONEY: £50.

THE BIG THREE

11

THEY WERE dubbed The Great Triumvirate and they bestrode the highest peaks of golf for two decades.

Of the 21 Opens played between 1894 and 1914, John Henry Taylor, Harry Vardon and James Braid won 16 of them - and of the five they didn't win, one or more of the trio finished runner-up

Only Harold Hilton (1897), Sandy Herd (1902), Jack White (1904), Arnaud Massy (1907) and Ted Ray (1912) managed, temporarily, to loosen their stranglehold.

To emphasise their dominance, The Big Three also won the nation's second most prestigious competition, the *News of the World* Match Play Championship, seven times in 10 events between 1903 and 1912.

Such was their near-monopoly of the game's top events that in 1903 *Golf Illustrated* magazine suggested that all professional tournaments other than the Open Championship should operate a handicap system, with the leading players playing off plus.

It would, the magazine said, "be fairer to the rank-and-file of the profession who have to content themselves with very small sums, often not sufficient to cover out-of-pocket expenses, while the big prizes go with somewhat regular monotony to one of three or four men."

The Professional Golfers' Association was even drawn into the discussion, but it was generally felt that if total prize funds for tournaments were increased the problem would quietly go away - and that is precisely what happened.

There is no clear consensus on how the title of Great Triumvirate originated, but, according to the golf writer, Bernard Darwin, it first

GOLF'S GREAT TRIUMVIRATE: Clement Flower's iconic painting of JH, left, and James Braid watching Harry Vardon drive from the tee. The trio were almost unbeatable between 1894-1914

PICTURE REPRODUCED BY KIND PERMISSION OF THE ROYAL AND ANCIENT GOLF CLUB OF ST ANDREWS

FLYING SCOT: James Braid, top left, racked up five Open Championships in ten years

HISTORY MAN: Harry Vardon, top right, stands alone with six Open triumphs

RELUCTANT HERO: JH, left, a five-time Open champion, had no time for the "Great Triumvirate" label

surfaced in a report of a match featuring the trio and the professional at South Herts Golf Club, in Totteridge, in 1901.

It was not, though, a soubriquet that sat comfortably with any of
the Big Three.

Taylor wrote: "That grandiloquent title was as repugnant to
Vardon and Braid as it was distasteful to me. It put us on a pedestal
of such eminence that it was scarcely fair to the rest of our fellow
players."

And he argued that Scotland's Herd, in particular, did not receive
the recognition he deserved: "As a trier, Sandy was one of the
hardest - I could mention others and because their names have not
headed the lists more frequently it should not deprive them of
being bracketed with the best.

"Professional golfers are loyal to each other and are pleased when
success comes to the fortunate, and the idea that a few are singled
out for excessive adulation is resented because of the spirit of com-
radeship that exists between them."

Be that as it may, the tag of Triumvirate was here to stay - and
history has confirmed that they really were the Special Ones.

Vardon, born in Grouville, on the Channel Island of Jersey in
1870, was one of two golfing brothers and popularised the over-
lapping grip that the Scottish amateur, Johnny Laidlay, had first
perfected. After spells at Studley Royal, Bury and Ganton in the
north of England, he moved to the South Herts club at Totteridge,
near London, as its professional in 1902 and remained there until
his death in 1937.

Vardon's feat of six Open victories, in 1896, 1898, 1899, 1903, 1911
and 1914, has never been equalled. The last of those triumphs, after
a dramatic final round at Prestwick, denied Taylor his last realistic
chance of reaching that historic milestone.

Vardon conquered America by winning the US Open in 1900,
finished second there in 1920 and, in between, lifted the inaugural
German Open title in 1911 and the *News of the World* Match Play in
1912.

He was, according to Taylor, quite simply the best and almost
certainly would have achieved even greater success had he not
been plagued by ill health, including tuberculosis, which required
lengthy stays in a sanatorium.

Braid, a 6ft 2in Scot from the Fife fishing village of Earlsferry, had moved to London to work as a club-maker at the Army & Navy Stores before making his mark in the game. He was appointed the professional at Romford, Essex, in 1896 and moved to Walton Heath, in Surrey, in 1903. He would remain there for 47 years until his death, aged 80, in 1950.

Braid's record of five victories between 1901 and 1910 - achieved in quicker time than Taylor or Vardon - is considered by many to be one of the finest achievements in Open history. To complete a remarkable sequence, he also won the Match Play title in 1903, 1905, 1907 and 1911, and the French Open in 1910.

Taylor wrote of Braid's first win, at Muirfield: "From now on the fame of Vardon and Taylor became associated with that of Braid and, speaking for myself as well as Vardon, the association welded itself into a most happy companionship that carried not a trace of envy with it."

In 1921, the Triumvirate played in the first Great Britain-United States "international" match at Gleneagles, with the American team comprising players who had come to Scotland for that year's Open at St Andrews. Britain won by nine matches to three, with three halved.

Following a similar match at Wentworth in 1926, Sam Ryder, a St Albans seed merchant and golf enthusiast, put up his famous trophy for the inaugural official contest in 1927. The Big Three selected the first British team that played at Worcester Country Club, Massachusetts, but did not pick themselves.

Throughout their exhibition careers between 1894 and 1914, Taylor and Vardon played each other 47 times, with Vardon winning 26, Taylor 19 and two halved. Taylor and Braid couldn't be separated in their 74 head-to-head meetings, each winning 31 matches with 12 halved.

Including Herd in his assessment, Taylor concluded: "To these three splendid pals I owe much of the pleasure that a hard professional life has afforded. The thought that we fought each other without bitterness or rancour on the links, at the same time sharing hopes and expressing doubts and delighting in each other's successes, remains with me a precious memory."

TAYLOR ON VARDON

JH Taylor's first close-up sighting of Harry Vardon came in a challenge match at Ganton in May, 1896, between the Hampshire and Isle of Wight Golf Association and the Yorkshire County Golf Union - believed to be the first inter-county match ever held. It was to be a chastening experience.

Taylor wrote: "Vardon's reputation had been growing steadily. He was being spoken of as one who was soon going to shake up all aspiring champions, but I was not greatly alarmed. I was soon to be undeceived - Vardon gave me one of the biggest hidings that I have ever received, by eight and seven.

"The match had not been going long before I realised that here was a player who was far above the ordinary. His placidity, his coolness, the unruffled nature of his game were such to unsettle a much less nervy player than me.

"In his early days, Harry had a most ungainly style. A lift in his back swing violated the principle of orthodoxy. One expected to see the ball slung far away to the right or sharply to the left, but, as if in defiance of all accepted standards, nothing of the sort happened.

"As the days went on, Vardon's lift became embodied in a style that was as graceful and perfect as any golf swing one is ever likely to see. Little did I guess at Ganton that day that I was playing a man who was to make golfing history and develop into - in my solemn and considered judgment - the finest and most finished golfer that the game has ever produced.

"I have long since been conscious that his demeanour towards his fellow men conformed to his high quality as a golf artist. There was a gentleness inherent in Vardon's conduct that reminded one of his easy persuasiveness when hitting the ball. Kindly, considerate and without harshness, he looked upon the world with tolerance and understanding and went on his way oblivious to the fact that, in him, was to be seen its greatest golfer."

ON Vardon's death in 1937, JH was asked to record an appreciation of his old friend and foe. Here is a transcript of his moving tribute:

"I am often asked whom I considered to be the best golfer ever I saw and with a life's experience behind me and having seen all the great players in 50 years I give it as my mature and considered judgment that Vardon was the greatest of them all.

"His style was so apparently simple that it was apt to mislead. It got its effect with that delightful effortless ease that was tantalising. It was a legend of the game that Vardon was never off the centre of any fairway in two years of play. I can scarcely subscribe to this, but I do say without fear of contradiction that he played fewer shots out of the rough than anyone who has ever swung a golf club. If the test of a good player be that he makes fewer bad shots than the remainder, then I give Vardon the part. To hit the ball with the centre of every club with greater frequency than any other player - in this most difficult feat lay his great strength as a player.

"In addition to his wonderful skill, Harry Vardon will be remembered as long as the game lasts as one of the most courteous and delightful opponents that ever could be. Throughout the years that I knew him I never heard him utter one disparaging remark about any other player. He will always be remembered as one of the most kindly souls that ever existed. To know him was to love him."

TAYLOR ON BRAID

"Jimmy's win (in 1901 at Muirfield) seemed to give him that confidence in his terrific powers which in succeeding years increased as much as the quality of his game improved."

"As a hitter of the ball, James has had no superior, and as a player up to the hole with any kind of iron club he challenges comparison with the best.

"Long, straight, beautifully-controlled driving, with rasping and ripping iron shots were to be expected, but it was his putting that placed him in his proud position.

"Like others who at some time have found themselves labelled weak in a particular stroke, James has had tacked on to him the reputation of a bad putter. This may have been justified in the early days and I will agree that he has always been frightened by the short putt - but what golfer that ever lived hasn't?

HOME FROM HOME: JH, left, with James Braid, Harry Vardon and RND professional Charles Gibson, second left, at Westward Ho!

FABULOUS FOUR: Sandy Herd, below right, with the Great Triumvirate, Taylor, left, Braid and Vardon

"But this supposed weakness is more than compensated by the exactitude of the long run-up approach putts. As a diviner of the true line to the hole, there is no superior and as a judge of strength he is in the front rank.

"James's rise to eminence in the putting game began when he first used an aluminium putter and discarded the weird and wonderful iron implements that all shaky holers-out use as a hoped-for corrective.

"Instead of a snappy, jerky action, he developed a smooth, slow take-back of the club and stroked rather than hit the ball towards the hole.

"His success engendered a great confidence which increased until he became one of the world's great putters, and I have yet to meet the player who could hole the 10-yard putts with greater regularity."

"James Braid is the most phlegmatic and least excitable person I have ever met. I have seen him excited, but his suppression of anything emotional gives the impression that any outward sign is childish and unworthy.

"Jimmy will, I know, forgive me if I attempt a little character sketch which my long years of acquaintanceship may warrant. I do it in very few words, because he hates verbosity. His loveable character can be summed up in three - sincerity, trustworthiness, loyalty. James is a man of few words. His reticence is but a cloak to hide his real feelings."

TAYLOR ON SANDY HERD

"Sandy was to Vardon what the exuberance of a whirlwind is to the soft caresses of a summer breeze. In playing, as in other things, Sandy put in every ounce of his fiery Scottish nature. There were never any half-measures.

"Unlike Vardon's quiet brand of friendship, or Braid's restraint in offering it, Sandy embodied in all he did the signs that he was asking for acceptance of what was worthwhile and, when reciprocity was assured, it could be taken for granted that it was based on mutual and enduring respect."

HARRY VARDON'S OPEN RECORD

Date	Venue	Rounds	Total	Position
1893	Prestwick	84 - 90 - 81 - 89	344	23
1894	Royal St George's, Sandwich	86 - 86 - 82 - 80	334	5
1895	St Andrews	80 - 85 - 85 - 88	338	9=
1896	Muirfield	83 - 78 - 78 - 77	316	1
1897	Royal Liverpool, Hoylake	84 - 80 - 80 - 76	320	6
1898	Prestwick	79 - 75 - 77 - 76	307	1
1899	Royal St George's, Sandwich	76 - 76 - 81 - 77	310	1
1900	St Andrews	79 - 81 - 80 - 77	317	2
1901	Muirfield	77 - 78 - 79 - 78	312	2
1902	Royal Liverpool, Hoylake	72 - 77 - 80 - 79	308	2=
1903	Prestwick	73 - 77 - 72 - 78	300	1
1904	Royal St George's, Sandwich	76 - 73 - 79 - 74	302	5
1905	St Andrews	80 - 82 - 84 - 83	329	9=
1906	Muirfield	77 - 73 - 77 - 78	305	3
1907	Royal Liverpool, Hoylake	84 - 81 - 74 - 80	319	7=
1908	Prestwick	79 - 78 - 74 - 75	306	5=
1909	Royal Cinque Ports, Deal	82 - 77 - 79 - 78	316	26=
1910	St Andrews	77 - 81 - 75 - 80	313	16=
1911	Royal St George's Sandwich	74 - 74 - 75 - 80	303	1
1912	Muirfield	75 - 72 - 81 - 71	299	2
1913	Royal Liverpool, Hoylake	79 - 75 - 79 - 80	313	3=
1914	Prestwick	73 - 77 - 78 - 78	306	1
1915-19	OPEN SUSPENDED DUE TO FIRST WORLD WAR			
1920	Royal Cinque Ports, Deal	78 - 81 - 81 -78	318	14=
1921	St Andrews	77 - 77 - 80 - 74	308	23=
1922	Royal St George's, Sandwich	79 - 79 - 74 - 75	307	8=
1923	Royal Troon	DID NOT PLAY		
1924	Royal Liverpool, Hoylake	DID NOT PLAY		
1925	Prestwick	79 - 80 - 77 - 79	315	17=
1926	Royal Lytham and St Annes	80 - 82 MISSED CUT		63
1927	St Andrews	78 - 78 MISSED CUT		76
1928	Royal St George's, Sandwich	78 - 79 - 80 - 80	317	47=
1929	Muirfield	82 - 78 MISSED CUT		78

JAMES BRAID'S OPEN RECORD

Date	Venue	Rounds	Total	Position
1894	Royal St George's, Sandwich	91 - 84 - 82 -84	341	10
1895	St Andrews	DID NOT PLAY		
1896	Muirfield	83 - 81 - 79 - 80	323	6
1897	Royal Liverpool, Hoylake	80 - 74 - 82 - 79	315	2
1898	Prestwick	80 - 82 - 84 - 75	321`	10=
1899	Royal St George's, Sandwich	78 - 78 - 85 - 81	322	5=
1900	St Andrews	82 - 81 - 80 - 79	322	3
1901	Muirfield	79 - 76 - 74 - 80	309	1
1902	Royal Liverpool, Hoylake	78 - 76 - 80 - 74	308	2=
1903	Prestwick	77 - 79 - 79 - 75	310	5
1904	Royal St George's, Sandwich	77 - 80 - 69 - 71	297	2
1905	St Andrews	81 - 78 - 78 - 81	318	1
1906	Muirfield	77 - 76 - 74 - 73	300	1
1907	Royal Liverpool, Hoylake	82 - 85 - 75 - 76	318	5=
1908	Prestwick	70 - 72 - 77 - 72	291	1
1909	Royal Cinque Ports, Deal	79 - 75 - 73 - 74	301	2=
1910	St Andrews	76 - 73 - 74 - 76	299	1
1911	Royal St George's, Sandwich	78 - 75 - 74 - 78	305	5=
1912	Muirfield	77 - 71 - 77 - 78	303	3
1913	Royal Liverpool, Hoylake	80 - 79 - 82 - 80	321	18=
1914	Prestwick	74 - 82 - 78 - 82	316	10=
1915-19	OPEN SUSPENDED DUE TO FIRST WORLD WAR			
1920	Royal Cinque Ports, Deal	79 - 80 - 79 - 82	320	21=
1921	St Andrews	77 - 75 - 78 - 76	306	16=
1922	Royal St George's, Sandwich	DID NOT PLAY		
1923	Royal Troon	79 - 85 - 79 -74	317	49=
1924	Royal Liverpool, Hoylake	80 - 80 - 78 - 76	314	18=
1925	Prestwick	DID NOT PLAY		
1926	Royal Lytham and St Annes	82 - 75 - 75 - 79	311	28=
1927	St Andrews	75 - 77 - 76 - 78	306	30=
1928	Royal St George's, Sandwich	80 - 79 - 81 - 76	316	41=
1938	Royal St George's, Sandwich	74 - 78 MISSED CUT		63=

FOR COMPLETE CHAMPIONSHIP RECORDS GO TO www.opengolf.com AND CLICK ON HISTORY

SINKING FEELING: JH takes a drop from the burn at the fourth hole - and his hopes of gaining an historic sixth Open win at the expense of Harry Vardon disappear at Prestwick in 1914

THE ONE THAT GOT AWAY

A RUSHED lunch break may have cost Taylor a record sixth Open victory.

He had turned a two-stroke halfway deficit into a two-shot lead after round three of his 1914 shoot-out with Harry Vardon at Prestwick.

"I had my digs at Troon and as a consequence of my lack of foresight was obliged to get my lunch as best I could close at hand," he wrote.

"On this critical occasion I found this makeshift policy a serious detriment and its hurried improvisation deprived me of the opportunity of rest and quiet reflection that was so necessary to the final effort.

"I do not put this forward as an excuse - it was my own fault - but I do own up to being a bit flustered when we got on to the tee to begin the last round."

Unsettled by the rush, Taylor missed a 2ft birdie putt on the first green that would have put him four strokes ahead - Vardon had taken a bogey five - and he then imploded on the fourth with a disastrous seven.

Taylor wrote: "The playing of the Pow Burn hole will remain with me for ever as a horrible recollection. . . it proved to be the greatest tragedy of my golfing life.

"Just before the Championship the clever James Braid had been called upon to tighten up the course, one result being that a couple of bunkers had been cunningly placed about where a reasonably good and straight drive would finish, leaving a horribly narrow passage between them and the edge of the burn.

"Vardon steered his drive splendidly between the hazards, which I tried to copy, but hitting the ball off the heel it meandered into a shallow bunker situated at the bend in the stream. When I reached the spot I found the ball lying clearly in the sand, presenting no great difficulty. I stepped into the bunker with no misgivings, but struck it heavily and spooned it out a few yards and into the burn. This meant a lift and a drop and the sorry tale must be told that I took three putts and an ugly seven went on the card."

Vardon, who had picked up a shot at the third hole, secured his four and was now one stroke ahead.

"What was even more lamentable," Taylor wrote, "was that my nerves had given way. A wave of nervous anxiety suddenly flooded my system, and the mischief was accomplished before I could conquer this feeling. . . suddenly I seemed to realise the importance of the occasion and all it meant to me, and for two or three holes I was absolutely helpless. After that I pulled myself together and was as cool as ice, but I had then lost my chance."

Vardon had the momentum he needed to close out the tournament - and his place in history - by three strokes.

Taylor lamented: "Had I succeeded with that first putt I think it would have made a vast difference to the final result."

IT SHOULD have been a marketing man's dream - three golfing superstars going head-to-head for the game's biggest prizes and a rapidly expanding fan base as the sport enjoyed an explosion in popularity.

A drift in population from the country to towns and cities, increased leisure time and even the advent of the longer-lasting - and therefore cheaper - Haskell ball all made golf more accessible to a wider public.

The estimated number of people playing golf rose almost eight-fold from 24,000 in 1898 to 185,000 a decade later, and tens of thousands more, though unable to play themselves, were increasingly keen to follow the fortunes of their heroes.

There was one problem - no television. Without television there was no money flooding into any form of sport from broadcasting rights and, without mass exposure, only limited opportunities to negotiate the equipment and clothing endorsements that today's multi-millionaires enjoy.

Quite simply, the Great Triumvirate were ahead of their time and golf, like all the major sports of the day, had to settle for its oxygen fix of publicity from the written word.

To be fair, the game was well served by a robust regional press and, from its launch in 1853, by regular coverage in the weekly *Field* magazine.

Country Life, another weekly focusing on golf and racing, hit the news stands in 1897 alongside *Golf* and *Golf Illustrated* and they all provided lively forums for debate. Taylor's early mentor, Horace Hutchinson, was also a prolific and respected writer in publications such as the *Badminton Library on Golf*.

But only three of today's mainstream English dailies, *The Times*, *The Daily Telegraph* and *The Guardian* - then *The Manchester Guardian* - were publishing when JH Taylor won his first Open in 1894, though *The Daily Mail*, in 1896, *The Daily Express* (1900) and *The Daily Mirror* (1903) soon followed.

The Observer, *The Sunday Times* and the *News of the World* - to which Taylor contributed a column for more than 40 years - offered weekend coverage, but JH, by and large, was singularly unimpressed by some of the early offerings from the gentlemen of the press.

It wasn't the quantity that bothered him - *The Times* report of the first day's play in his Open triumph at Sandwich in 1894, published the following morning, ran to more than 2,500 words, but it was little more than a litany of names and scores.

Taylor observed in his autobiography. "I have been in the game long enough to remember the perfunctory manner in which golf matches were reported. There was no detailed description of the play, nothing to excite the imagination or to quicken the pulse, nothing but a bare recital of the number of strokes taken at each hole, of wins, losses or halves."

SUPER SCRIBE: JH's friend, Bernard Darwin

But that changed in 1907 when *The Times* appointed Bernard Darwin as its first full-time golf writer.

An accomplished amateur golfer himself, Darwin had qualified as a barrister, but after a short spell practising law he decided that life on the fairways was a more satisfying option.

Darwin, who never trained as a journalist, brought a new dimension to the way golf was reported, both in the columns of his own newspaper and the pages of *Country Life*, to which he contributed for more than 50 years.

As was the custom at *The Times*, Darwin wrote anonymously under the byline of "Our Golf Correspondent", but there was no mistaking his style.

Taylor, who enjoyed a life-time friendship with Darwin, enthused: "He has gained the enviable reputation of being the finest writer on the game. He was the first to introduce human touches and shrewd comments, enabling one to visualise the scene and sense the drama.

"Mr Darwin is equipped to write on golf as no other man. By his high degree of playing skill, his deep knowledge of and

The New York Times

J. H. TAYLOR QUITS GOLF

Five Times British Open Champion Retires from Competition.

Copyright, 1920, by The New York Times Company.

Special Cable to THE NEW YORK TIMES.

LONDON, June 22.—J. H. Taylor, five times open golf champion of Great Britain, is retiring at the age of 50, because, he says, " the young man of today is too strong for me. He hits the ball too far. I can't keep up with him."

BUNKERED: The boys at *The New York Times* got a little ahead of the game with this premature report in 1920

---

acquaintance with golf and golfers in the early vintage days and, above all, by his literary excellence, his writing is peerless."

Herbert Warren Wind, the former player and American writer who coined the phrase "Amen Corner" at Augusta, said: "Once Darwin dipped his toe into golf writing, the reports he produced regularly for *The Times* and his ruminative essays for *Country Life* possessed a quality that no-one else has ever approached."

Ben Crenshaw, a double Masters champion and student of golf history, wrote: "To me, he appealed to the reader on the most individualistic terms. He talked to us, apologised to us, cried to us, bared his temper to us, and made us laugh with him, all in an attempt to reveal his deep, deep love for golf to us."

The written word of golf was now in the most talented of hands - but there was still no television.

As Taylor and his peers sat in retirement with tournament prize funds rising and the public's fixation with sport reaching new heights, wasn't there the slightest feeling that they had been dealt a rough hand?

Taylor wrote in his book: "When I consider the big rewards and prizes provided these days I sometimes wish that I had been born 30 years later. On reflection, it is a churlish wish, for had I been I would have missed the companionship of a splendid band of professionals of my generation, who, if I may express it, laid the foundation for the chivalry and good conduct existing among all golf professionals today."

Fine words, but none of his generation of sporting superstars would have been human if they hadn't thought: "What if. . ."

• JH TAYLOR was no mean writer himself and became a sought-after contributor to newspapers and magazines even beyond his retirement from golf in 1946.

In addition to his role as a columnist for the *News of the World*, he regularly wrote articles for the specialist golf magazines and other periodicals of the day.

Along with some of his peers, he also collaborated with George Beldam - a Middlesex cricketer and talented amateur photographer credited by some as the inventor of sports action photography - by providing the words for picture-led instructional columns and strips.

ACE OF CLUBS

12

I T WAS what JH called "a dude" among golf clubs - bold and original - and it played a key role in three Open title triumphs. John Henry Taylor's signature club, the mashie, became almost as famous as the man himself.

He had acquired it in 1888 after finishing second in a competition staged by the Northam Working Men's Golf Club.

The prizes had been donated by Royal North Devon members - and Taylor's reward was the club of his choice from the pro shop.

Charles Gibson, the RND professional, steered him towards a sample club he had just received from the Scottish club-maker, Anderson of Anstruther.

It was a new type of club, Gibson said, that they called a "mashie", something between an iron and a niblick.

It was love at first sight.

Taylor wrote: "Directly I handled it, I felt it would suit me. It had a short, squat head, deep in face with about the loft of a well-set back iron and had a hickory shaft fitted to it like a young tree.

"I visualised that it could be used for getting out of bunkers or playing delicate chip shots from just off the green or, greatly daring, used for approach play.

"Hitherto, we played the shot up to the hole with a lofting iron which, although at times effective, gave too much margin for error owing to its long blade.

"This 'mashie', I thought, could be successfully used to pitch shots up to the hole from about 80 yards.

Taylor believed the club drew its name from the term "masher" which apparently applied to "those ultra-smart young fellows who,

FAITHFUL FRIEND: JH confounded his critics by winning his first three Opens with the mashie club which he won as second prize in a club competition. The club, pictured left and below, now resides in the Royal North Devon Golf Club museum. JH's final two Opens were won with his own Cann and Taylor version of the mashie

PUTTING ON THE STYLE: Pictured right is the hickory-shafted, aluminium head putter that JH Taylor used in his Open triumphs of 1909 and 1913. It was also in his bag when he won the French Open in 1909 and the German Open three years later. It now forms part of the memorabilia collection at the Professional Golfers' Association headquarters at The Belfry.

PICTURE COURTESY OF THE PGA

with monocle in eye and arrayed in clothes of the latest style and cut, were the idol of every lady.

"Whether this was so or not, I do not know, but I do know that the new-fashioned club was considered to be a violent departure from the orthodox, a dude among clubs, so what better name could be given it than the 'mashie', a parody on the popular conception of smartness?"

It was a faithful ally in the Taylor bag for 12 years, confounding the critics who said it would be a liability on hard greens like those at St Andrews, but eventually it had to be discarded - the club face now uneven through constant cleaning with an emery cloth.

"I did so with feelings of real regret," said Taylor. "It had been my staunch friend in many a difficulty, though I look at it now and wonder that such a clumsy weapon was ever capable of doing what it accomplished."

Taylor would win two more Opens, in 1909 and 1913, with a mashie made by Cann and Taylor, the club-making arm of Taylor's business portfolio. The company sold thousands of their version of the club - but JH never lost his affection for his beloved Anderson of Anstruther "dude".

IT IS 1902 and the arguments had raged for months in the pages of *Golf Illustrated* - the gutty or the Haskell.

The traditional gutty golf ball made from the sap of the gutta tree had superseded the old "featherie" in the 1850s.

Now it was under threat from a new pretender - rubber thread wrapped around a solid rubber core - that had been pioneered by the American Coburn Haskell and Bertram Work, an employee of the Goodrich company in Ohio.

John Henry Taylor had seen the future back in 1900 - but confessed to being too conservative to take the risk. He had spurned the chance to use the Haskell that year at the US Open in Wheaton, Illinois, saying: "It might put me off my touch and that, on the eve of a Championship, would likely prove more harmful than gunpowder with a lighted fuse."

But subsequent trial rounds with the new ball after the tournament - when he committed the unpardonable "sin" of driving into the group in front because he did not think he would reach them - convinced him that the days of the gutty were numbered.

As the debate intensified, most of Taylor's peers stood squarely behind the gutty: JH was looked on as an alarmist imbued with American ideas.

The main complaints against the Haskell were that it was difficult to control on approach shots, would not hold its line on the greens and was susceptible to splitting.

As the 1902 Open drew near, Sandy Herd, the Scottish professional, observed: "I think the Haskell ball is very difficult to play with. It drives all right, but that is about all I can say about it. What one thinks he can gain in the drive, he will very soon lose on the putting green. It is too fiery altogether on the green. I hope all the professionals play with it at Hoylake except myself."

Harry Vardon went further, weighing in with the prediction that no-one using the Haskell would win that year's Open.

The debate would be settled in almost farcical fashion.

Herd was playing his final practice round when his partner, the amateur Johnnie Ball, plucked a dilapidated Haskell from his pocket - thread hanging from the ball - and tossed it to Herd to try. He was so impressed with the results that he decided there and then to use it in the Championship the next day.

Herd - the sole player in the field using a Haskell - won his only Open title.

The argument would continue to rage, but, to all intents and purposes, Herd's victory sounded the death knell for the gutty.

FOUNDING FATHER
OF THE PGA

13

I T WAS the moment when golf's hard-pressed professionals finally decided that enough was enough. Around the turn of the last century, some employers, quick to cash in on the game's rapidly increasing popularity, began to put the club-making and ball business that was traditionally the domain of the club professionals out to the highest bidder.

The move would have dealt a crushing blow to the livelihoods of the sitting pros - and, understandably, it brought an avalanche of protest.

It would also unleash a chain of events - with John Henry Taylor in the vanguard - that would revolutionise the game of golf.

Faced with a storm of opposition from golfers, the game's authorities and the golfing press, the clubs dramatically backed down - but the furore was just the wake-up call the game needed.

Famously, a letter from an unnamed "North Wales professional" to *Golf Illustrated* on April 12, 1901, urged that "the time was now ripe to band themselves into an association to promote the general welfare of the professional and look after his interests."

Another letter from a North of England professional agreed, but argued that any such move would be "doomed to failure" unless it had the backing of the game's leading players.

The articulate Taylor - "by common opinion among all professionals their ideal leader," according to the North Wales correspondent - needed no second invitation.

In his own letter to *Golf Illustrated* he had condemned the policy as "likely to return the professional to the state of comparative poverty common not a great many years ago."

By September, 1901, with the endorsement of other leading players including James Braid and Harry Vardon, JH had galvanised enough support to form the London and Counties Golf Professionals' Association.

Its aims were "to promote interest in the game of golf; to protect and advance the mutual and trade interests of all its members; to hold meetings and tournaments periodically for the encouragement of younger members; to institute a Benevolent Fund for the relief of deserving members; and to act as an agency for assisting any professional or club-maker to obtain employment".

Taylor was elected chairman and Braid, the current Open champion, captain. With a simple name change agreed at the group's first annual meeting on December 2, 1901, and an initial membership of 59 professionals and 11 assistants, The Professional Golfers' Association was born.

As other regional associations threw their hats in with the new body, the PGA quickly provided a powerful platform for all professionals, club-makers and assistants throughout the country.

But it was not a trade union. While one of the key objectives was to protect the interests of its members, the focus was on welfare, not industrial relations.

The establishment of a Benevolent Fund for members who had fallen sick or on hard times and the creation of a register for those offering and seeking work were just as important as members' rights or developing new tournaments.

For Taylor, the PGA became a lifelong commitment as chairman, captain and executive committee member. He brought a voice of reason to the big issues of the day, balancing the needs of his fellow professionals against the wider interests of the game.

There was one moment that might have forced him to "consider his position" within the Association when some of his colleagues sought to stop the leading players from supporting golf promotions at stores like Harrods, but the ban never materialised.

The hiccup over, Taylor continued to throw himself into the work of the PGA and his contributions were honoured first with an invitation to captain the 1933 Ryder Cup team and, in 1949, with his election as a Vice President.

JH TAYLOR'S contribution to the PGA was formally recognised in 1949 when he was elected a Vice President. The commendation read:

"WE, all members of the Professional Golfers' Association, desire to place on record our admiration, esteem and appreciation to you for your long and faithful services given to the promotion and advancement of our profession and the good of golf generally.

"We tender our congratulations to you upon being elected a Vice President of our Association and we thank you for accepting this signal Honour, so richly deserved. We express the hope that we, and the whole golfing world, will enjoy the benefit of your company and wisdom over a great many years, knowing well that you will retain the highest respect and esteem of all."

The commendation was signed by the PGA Chairman, Arthur J Lacey, and the Secretary, Commander Charles Roe.

Few, if any, of those present at that inaugural meeting in 1901 could have imagined the influence that the PGA would come to exert today as one of the leading bodies within the sport.

From its humble origins, the PGA now has more than 7,500 members and a network of contacts that stretches across the globe.

Much of the credit for this success belongs to Commander Charles Roe, who was appointed secretary in 1934 and remained at the helm for 28 years.

Roe, who enjoyed the complete support of Taylor, almost certainly inspired more respect for his achievements than he did affection for his autocratic leadership style, but no-one should underestimate his impact on the PGA and its standing in golf.

He regulated the membership, balanced the books and, as a retired naval commander, was able to move comfortably among the high fliers of commerce and industry as he sought to persuade them to sponsor tournaments or invest in other PGA initiatives.

When Roe climbed on board, there were just nine tournaments - only one organised by the PGA - with a total prize fund of £7,000. He also had to go cap-in-hand to his business friends to finance the 1935 Ryder Cup trip to New Jersey.

By the time he left, there were 19 tournaments with a prize pot of more than £75,000 - all but one under PGA jurisdiction - and there was more than £20,000 in the Ryder coffers.

Ironically, the growth of tournaments that began under Roe continued at such a pace that it proved to be a double-edged sword for the PGA.

Finding it increasingly difficult to juggle the needs of its traditional club professionals with those of the tournament players, the Association created a separate Tournament Division in 1974 and ten years later this evolved into the autonomous European Tour.

The PGA continues to support and promote tournament play at every level below the Tour, but undoubtedly the jewel in the crown remains the Ryder Cup.

As trustee of the original trophy donated by Sam Ryder in 1926, the Association is a key partner in what has become one of the biggest events in global sport.

The PGA also plays a significant role in the development of golf - from junior coaching through to government level, where it is helping formulate policy for the sport. This programme includes active involvement with the England Golf Partnership's Whole Sport Plan, Club Golf Scotland, Golf Development Wales, Junior Golf Ireland and the implementation of the UK Coaching Certificate for golf.

Now based at its plush headquarters at The Belfry, near Birmingham, the PGA has come a long way since that momentous day back in 1901. Taylor wrote in his autobiography in 1943: "The

THE FIRST tournament held under the auspices of the PGA - The Tooting Bec Cup - was staged in October, 1901.

To be strictly accurate, the event was organised by the London and Counties Golf Professionals' Association, which had been formed a month earlier - that body would change its name to the Professional Golfers' Association at its first annual meeting in December of the same year.

Peter Paxton, runner-up in the 1880 Open Championship and professional at the Tooting Bec club, had chaired the meeting at which the London association was founded and his club was asked to host the inaugural 36-hole stroke play competition.

Happy to oblige, Tooting also agreed to put up the trophy. The tournament had a total prize fund of £15 and it was perhaps fitting that the first holder of the cup - and winner by three strokes of the £5 top prize - should be none other than the Association's founding father, John Henry Taylor.

PGA became of some importance in the world of golf, content to look after its members and giving them a status that was not previously enjoyed.

"Some harsh words have occasionally been used by the unthinking about the Association's activities, implying disloyalty to the authorities that govern the game.

"If my word can be believed, I can say that while it has watched and still continues to watch over the interests of the professional, the Association has never set itself in such a way as to oppose in a revolutionary or vindictive spirit anything that would forfeit its good name. I am proud to have helped build it."

David Wright, Heritage Executive at the PGA, puts it more succinctly: "Harry Vardon and James Braid played their part, but JH Taylor stood above them by a long way. He was the driving force, he was the founding father of the PGA."

• *We are grateful to the PGA for allowing us to use extracts from its fascinating Centenary book, co-written by Richard Holt, Peter N Lewis and Wray Vamplew.*

ROSS DANIEL, the assistant at Royal North Devon, is just embarking on the PGA's Foundation Degree course in professional golf studies.

Nurturing the next generation of golf professionals has always been a key function of the Association, but the latest three-year course reflects how far the game has progressed in the past 100 years.

That progression gathered pace during the 1960s and 70s when the PGA revamped its training and education programme so that assistant professionals could gain qualifications in their chosen field and become businessmen in the world of professional golf.

By 2005 the training programme had taken on degree status in co-operation with the University of Birmingham and the aspiring golf professional would graduate with a Foundation Degree in professional golf studies covering all aspects of the game: playing, coaching and business skills.

More recently, a reshaping of the golfing landscape has seen the advent of new and more expansive managerial roles within golf complexes, golf resorts and driving ranges - and the PGA has adapted to ensure that its Members are properly qualified to meet

FAMOUS FOOTSTEPS: Ross Daniel, right, is starting out in golf at the RND club where JH Taylor began his illustrious journey in the game

all the challenges of a multi-million pound industry. Ross, 19, who is learning his trade under the watchful eyes of PGA Professionals Iain Parker and Mike Wilson at Royal North Devon, is confident he will acquire all the skills he needs to pursue a career in the sport. He said: "We still learn the basics of club repairs, teaching and running the professional's shop, but there is much more involved as well. The course includes equipment technology, sports science, including subjects like bio-mechanics, how to avoid injuries and advice on nutrition and business management, not just for the pro shop but golf complexes as a whole

"It also focuses on career and personal development, knowledge of the Rules and Tournament organisation.

"I'm looking forward to the course and really enjoy working at Royal North Devon. I've always wanted to be involved in golf.

"My ambition is to be as good as I can at everything I do. I'm proud of the fact that I'm starting out at the same club where JH Taylor took his first steps in golf. And if I could win five Opens . . . well, I think I might be satisfied with that!"

THE PEOPLE'S CHAMPION 14

JOHN HENRY TAYLOR was no class warrior. He respected the rights of the rich and the privileged who inhabited early golf society and, pragmatically, had no desire to usurp the powers of the influential "masters" who made such a significant contribution to his earning power.

But he also believed passionately in the right of ordinary folk to share the joys of the game he loved.

Taylor had been banging the drum as early as 1905, writing in *Golf Illustrated*: "Public links must come to London; there will be an outcry for them. Then we shall be able to tap a section of society which in other places has always proved most productive in skill in athletics and games.

"I mean the lower middle-class, comprising clerks and shopmen among others. The game would be a great boon to them, but they have not the means to enter London golf clubs in the present day, and they would not be admitted to them if they had.

"But their day will surely come, when every man who can afford to pay a five-shilling (25p) subscription will have his golf. If I said what I thought would be the position held by golf in, say, 20 years from now, I might be accused of too great optimism and of the wildest fancy. So we shall wait and see."

Taylor never lost the faith. In the twilight of his tournament career and with the country returning to some normality after the First World War, he set about fulfilling his vision of golf for everyone in the community.

Two direct results of his campaign - the founding of the Artisan Golfers' Association in 1921 and the formation of the National Association of Public Golf Courses in 1927 - would change the face

GOLD STANDARD: John Henry with his first medal, which he won at the age of 17 playing off scratch in a Northam Working Men's Club meeting in 1888.   PICTURE: BATH'S PHOTOGRAPHIC

144

of golf in Britain by bringing the game within reach of tens of thousands of working-class people.

They also sat perfectly with his personal belief that the playing of all sports would not just benefit the health of the nation but, at the same time, help to cure some of its social problems.

Taylor - joined every step of the journey by his friend and kindred spirit, the course designer Frederic George Hawtree - had no doubts about the justice of his mission.

As a founder member of Northam Working Men's Golf Club in 1888, he "remembered with gratitude" how the club had given him not just his first taste of competitive golf but had also provided a much-needed focal point for meeting new friends.

He had seen how schemes for cheap golf were operating successfully in Scotland and enthused about how the game was developing across the Atlantic.

"In America," he wrote, "I have met on municipal golf courses hundreds of working men who are true gentlemen, mechanics who have all the attributes of the highest kind of man, labourers who are as good fellows as any you will meet with in a day's march. They have all learned to manage their lives on right lines."

Before the First World War, Taylor had been commissioned by London County Council to lay out a public course at Hainault Forest, in Essex, which, though not the most accessible of areas, had proved to be very popular.

He considered it "little short of a disgrace that London was so ill-provided with public courses" - and, through the Artisan Golfers' Association, set out to rectify the situation.

Taylor's dedication to the project personified his entire commitment to the cause of public golf.

Having identified Richmond Park as a potential site, Taylor began to build a campaign team.

With Hawtree already on board, JH again enlisted the support of Lord Riddell, who had taken a prominent role in the establishment of the Professional Golfers' Association 20 years earlier.

He found another ally in Lord Northcliffe, owner of the *Daily Mail*. The pair had previously met as lunch guests of a mutual friend and, remembering being slightly surprised by the strength of

Northcliffe's support for the principle of golf for all, he wrote to the newspaper outlining his vision.

The campaign was now gathering a head of steam - but the first meeting with Government bureaucrats to discuss the plan in the spring of 1922 was less than promising.

Richmond was a Royal Park and, as such, came under the aegis of HM Office of Works.

Its First Commissioner, Lord Crawford, couldn't have been more blunt: the plan was out of the question; it would be dangerous to the general public and, anyway, there were irrevocable statutory powers in place that would prevent it.

All looked lost - until a timely intervention from Sir Lionel Earle, Permanent Secretary to the Office of Works.

There was, it transpired, a piece of ground outside the park proper where it might be possible to lay out a golf course.

If it did prove to be suitable, the Office would consider the proposal - but there would not be a penny of public money to finance the scheme.

Taylor, wasting no time, inspected the potential site the following day and discovered 96 acres of land just perfect for golf.

With the backing of £4,000 in loans from benefactors, official permission granted and rent agreed at £200 a year, Taylor and Hawtree set about designing the course and overseeing the construction of a club pavilion. A crowd of more than 2,000 looked on as HRH The Prince of Wales officially opened the course on June 6, 1923.

London had a new public golf facility - the first in a Royal Park - and the green fees were a very affordable 1s 6d (7.5p) for a round, 2s 6d (12.5p) for the day.

Taylor wrote later: "From all parts of London hundreds of players, and those desirous of learning how to play, came to the course to enjoy not only the pleasure it gave but also its beautiful surroundings."

In fact, demand was so great that the organising committee began looking for a second site within the park for another 18-hole course.

With Labour now in power, it was thought official approval would be a simple matter, but the new First Commissioner, Mr Frederick Jowett MP, initially seemed even more intractable than his predecessor, though the course was eventually sanctioned at a greatly increased rent.

Almost two years to the day after the first course was opened, The Duke of York followed his brother in making the ceremonial drive off the first tee.

By now, the Office of Works had invoked a clause inserted during negotiations for the original course that it would take over the management of the project at a future date "if desirable or expedient."

If this last act left a slightly bad taste for Taylor, it did not diminish his sense of achievement in establishing the two Richmond courses. "It was," he said, "something of which I shall always feel more than a little proud."

He could be rightly proud, too, of his dedicated service to the Professional Golfers' Association, the Artisan Golfers' Association and the National Association of Public Golf Courses - "a trio of organisations I had helped to found and whose activities I believe have done much towards adding to the pleasure of thousands of golfers all over the country."

TEE-OFF: The Duke of York hits the first drive at the official opening of the second public golf course in Richmond Park in 1925 as John Henry Taylor, left, the pioneer of the project, looks on

THE OPENING of Taylor's new course in Richmond Park created quite a stir, as this delightful report in the *Surrey Comet* on June 13, 1923, reveals:

THE PRINCE OF WALES AND GOLF

Auspicious Opening of the New Public Course in Richmond Park

H.R.H. Drives the First Ball

Over 2,000 People Witness the Ceremony

Just after 11 o'clock on Saturday morning the Prince of Wales drove the first ball on Richmond Park's new public golf course, a distance of about 30 yards at a cost of £1, and from Monday anyone who felt so inclined has been able to follow him at a much smaller cost.

Eagerly anticipated, the opening ceremony was watched by a gathering of between two and three thousand, of whom women were in the majority, and the "scene of action," the clubhouse, presented a very pretty aspect for the occasion. Bright with new green paint, decorated with a shield bearing the Prince of Wales' feathers and motto between a Union Jack and a White Ensign, and gay with rows of flowers, geraniums, pansies and daisies, the pavilion was crowded with members of the committee, their wives and friends a good three-quarters of an hour before the ceremony was due to begin, while in the reserved enclosure roped off in front, the people, many of whom were armed with cameras, jostled and pushed, eight and nine rows deep.

Members of the public, admitted by another gate, flowed in with a rush and occupied all the extra space that was available, while another large gathering collected at the main gates, where a fleet of motor cars was parked.

Dull and overcast up to that time, at a few minutes to eleven the sun shone out, a happy augury said many, and punctually to the minute, to the sound of cheering at the gates, the Prince's car swept up the drive and stopped at the side of the club house, where His Royal Highness, who was dressed in a grey check lounge suit with black tie and bowler hat and attended by Wing-Commander Louis Greig, was received by Sir John Baird, the First Commissioner of Works.

To the accompaniment of much cheering, the Prince walked to the steps of the club house where Sir John presented to him the members of the committee, with each of whom he shook hands. With Lord Riddell as chairman, the other members were Sir Joseph Hood, M.P., Sir Sydney Skinner, Sir Howard

148

Frank, Sir James Dunn, Mr. Leonard H. Bentall and Mr. G.W. Beldam, and Messrs. W. Leitch, D.N. Dyke and H. Ryle (representatives of the Office of Works on the committee), Mr. J.H.Taylor and Captain A.Smith (the secretary) and Josh Taylor, the professional of the course. Sir John also presented Mr. F.G. Penny, the M.P. for Kingston, to the Prince.

Origin of the Project

Introductions over, Sir John gave a short résumé of the reasons which led to the Office of Works granting permission for the construction of the course and, addressing the Prince, said they regarded it as a great honour that he had found it possible to come and open the first public golf course in a Royal park. As captain of the Royal and Ancient Golf Club, the senior club in the British Isles, it was also singularly appropriate that he should perform the ceremony, and they all thanked him very much.

The question of a golf course in the Park had been raised as far back as 1909 by the Mayor of Richmond, who wanted a course for those who could not afford to pay the subscriptions of an ordinary club. Further efforts were made in 1913 and 1921, and in the latter year the Artisan Golfers' Association approached his predecessor and, with the assistance of Lord Riddell, the scheme was formulated, and His Majesty gladly assented to facilities being afforded to people to play golf who were not perhaps in a financial position to play elsewhere. The result was a very fine course where anyone could play for 1s 6d a round. Nobody had been deprived of using the park, as where the course had been constructed was previously grazing land and inaccessible to the general public.

The Financial Backing

It was base ingratitude on his part to worry the Prince with another speech, said Lord Riddell, but he wanted to say that the course was in a large measure due to the efforts of the Artisan Golfers' Association. That perhaps was not a happy name, as it seemed to indicate that the members only worked with their hands, whereas it was to provide cheap golf both for those who worked with their hand and heads...

They were much obliged to the Office of Works for all they had done, but the course would not have been possible but for the financial help of Sir James Dunn, Sir Howard Frank, Sir Joseph Hood, Sir Sydney Skinner, Mr. Bentall, Mr Beldam, and, if he might say so, himself.

It was also right to state that it was in a tremendous degree due to J.H. Taylor (applause) who had done so much for golf and golfers all his life. It was due to Taylor, who had designed the course, that it was what it was now. (Applause.)

The Prince's Speech

Received with much enthusiasm, the Prince said it was a great pleasure to come and open the course which began a new era in the history of golf. It was the first of its kind to be completed, but he hoped that there would soon be many more like it, and that golf would soon become as universal and national game as football or cricket. There was no better recreation, after the day's work, whether with hand or head, than a game of golf, especially in such charming surroundings as these. The whole idea was a splendid one, well carried out.

"And now," concluded the Prince, to the music of many cameras "registering" him, "before I break the record for the first hole I should like to congratulate all those who are responsible for the course, those who thought of it and those whose generosity provided the necessary funds. I wish the course every possible success and a very long future."

H R H Drives Off

Speeches over, the Prince, accompanied by his equerry, members of the committee and Mr. J.H. Taylor, with the crowd surging about them, more or less pushed their way to the first tee. Here, looking distinctly nervous, he laid down his hat and stick, and accepting a driver form the hands of Josh Taylor, then took a few practice swings.

"Ladies and gentlemen," announced Mr. J. H. Taylor, "the Prince desires me to say that he will present a golden sovereign to the person who retrieves and returns the ball." This was greeted with loud cheers.

Tense silence then, as the ball was teed up by the veteran Mid-Surrey professional, and an elongated square pressed forward against the straining rope barrier in imminent danger if the ball flew far, and bang, as club head met rubber, the ball, topped and pulled, ricocheted off the foot of a spectator and bounded up the fairway about 30 yards from the tee. "What a rotten shot!" said the Prince as men and women flew after the ball. The proud finder was Mr. E. T. Willison, a railway employee of Oruro, Bolivia, South America, who is at present in this country on holiday and residing at Clapham.

Cap and ball in hand, he rushed up to the Prince, who shook hands with him and presented him with his reward. The ball was then given to Mr. J. H. Taylor, for whom it will be mounted as a memento by the committee. Mr. Taylor afterwards handed to Mr. Willison a golf ball on which he had written his signature.

After three hearty cheers had been given for him, and followed by the cheering crowd, the Prince slowly made his way back to his car, entering which he drove off to the Duke of York's residence, White Lodge, while the spectators of the ceremony, which from start to finish had lasted barely 15 minutes, strolled over the course and looked around the clubhouse.

THE Artisan Golfers' Association began life in 1921 at Anderton's Hotel, in Fleet Street, London.

With JH Taylor as a vice-president and fellow founding member Frederic George Hawtree as secretary, the new movement quickly struck a chord with the golfing public.

Having absorbed the old Working Men's Golf Clubs at its inception, by 1934 the original AGA membership of 30 clubs with 800 members had blossomed to 143 clubs representing 10,000 golfers.

The founding fathers had helped to form 60 of these clubs.

The association's status was confirmed that same year when an application by Hawtree and Taylor to join the English Golf Union was unanimously accepted, receiving the unqualified support of the EGU president, HRH The Prince of Wales.

Although membership has fallen in recent times, the AGA continues to be an influential voice within the sport.

Ninety years after JH set the ball rolling in Richmond, a new artisan club is scheduled to open in the royal park in 2011, while regulations that previously excluded artisan golfers from certain competitions are being relaxed.

Artisan clubs have their own club rooms, committees and tournaments, both local and national, but they do not own their own courses. Instead they use those of larger, traditionally-established clubs.

Some have been able to invoke local by-laws or ancient manorial rights to gain acceptance.

When JH Taylor and his colleagues founded the Northam Working Men's Golf Club in 1888, they could quote the Northam Award of 1716 that gave all "potwallopers" - ratepayers within

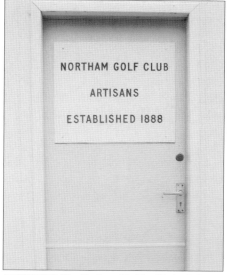

NEW DAWN: The Northam Working Men's Golf Club was the first of its kind in England

the manor of Northam and Appledore - "equal rights of grazing, air, exercise and recreation."

Under the Award, the Royal North Devon club, officially founded on the Burrows common land in 1864, was required to give the Working Men free use of the course.

But they were only allowed to play early in the morning or later in the afternoon - and they had to use a separate gate so that they did not walk in front of the clubhouse!

The Artisan Golfers' Association has always been keen to acknowledge its debt to John Henry Taylor. He was made president of the association in 1934 and a plaque donated by the AGA recognising the contribution of Taylor - and his financial backers - in opening the two Royal Park courses in 1923 and 1925 sits in the Richmond Park clubhouse.

The AGA also helped to perpetuate the memory of its founding father at his home church in Northam, of which more later.

§

THE National Association of Public Golf Courses was founded in 1927 by JH Taylor and his business partner, Frederic George Hawtree, the famous course architect.

Both men were passionate champions of golf for the masses and they sought to bring cohesion between public and private golf - a philosophy that remains unchanged.

Among other famous people involved in the birth of the association was Sir Emsley Carr, owner and editor of the *News of the World*, who would later become president. The current holder of that position is Sir Michael Bonallack OBE, the five-times British amateur champion and former secretary of the Royal and Ancient Golf Club.

An entirely voluntary organisation, the association's founding objectives were to promote annual championships and tournaments and to afford direct representation on the national golf union.

It was not easy in the early days to gain acceptance from the game's governing bodies but, by being seen to be a responsible and effective organisation, the association earned its right to be recognised by The Royal and Ancient Golf Club and the English Golf Union.

CHAMPION: Danny Elliott, from the Farnham Park Golf Club, Buckinghamshire, the 2010 winner of the NAPGC Men's Scratch Championship, is pictured with the JH Taylor Shield

With a current membership of around 100 affiliated golf clubs and a playing membership of some 25,000, the NAPGC has continued to grow as more clubs recognise the advantages of membership and competing in some of the nation's oldest and most competitive individual and team events.

To help maintain that expansion, the association opened its doors to include "proprietary" golf clubs and their members - from

January, 2009, it changed its name to the National Association of Public and Proprietary Golf Courses/Clubs

To explain the difference, public courses are municipally owned, but members form their own club and are in charge of their destiny; "proprietary" clubs are commercial or management owned, with members selecting their committee. Most proprietary clubs also allow pay-and-play golf.

A NAPGC survey, conducted with the help of the Bournemouth University Students Alliance, found there are about 450 public and proprietary clubs and courses in England and Wales, of which only 98 - around 22 per cent - are affiliated members.

The association has staged a series of meetings and presentations - including a CD with voice-over by Peter Alliss - to try to convince non-member clubs of the benefits of joining the NAPGC as full members.

The association's most prestigious tournament is the UK Public Course Championship, which attracts entries from the other home unions and reaches its climax over St Andrews in September.

For many years the *News of the World* financed the Challenge Cup and also presented the JH Taylor Shield, an important part of its Men's Championships, the finals of which are played at Woodhall Spa, the headquarters of the English Golf Union.

The EGU Championship Committee recently recognised the importance of the NAPGC scratch championship by offering the winner a place in the Champion of Champions event.

The Ladies' Championship finals were held in 2010 at the Abbotsley course in Cambridgeshire, while the Junior Championship, a very popular competition, has been played over the Tamworth course since the event's inception in 1977.

JH Taylor was elected president of the association in 1952 and held the position for four years.

• *We would like to thank Patrick Cunningham, vice president of the Artisan Golfers' Association, and Ken Whiteway, press officer for the National Association of Public and Proprietary Golf Courses/Clubs, for their invaluable help in compiling this chapter.*

SAVING THE NATION

15

J H TAYLOR was a deep thinker, a man of strong opinions who, when pressed, was not afraid to voice them. He fervently believed that the playing of games - any sport, not just his beloved golf - would cure the social ills that he considered had beset the nation after the First World War.

Here, during a golfing trip with his friend Harold Begbie in 1925, Taylor certainly doesn't hold back.

Begbie's account of their conversation in his book, *JH Taylor or The Inside of a Week*, conveys the trenchancy of Taylor's views - though, as his grandson John Taylor explained earlier, the strident tone of his language was not something with which he readily identified:

❛ I dare not contemplate what my life would have been, or what my nature may have become, if it had not been for the part played in my career, and in my soul, by the great game of golf.

I expect you have often heard it said that we Englishmen are too fond of our games and not half serious enough about our work. It is urged against us that we have lost the tremendous earnestness of our forefathers which enabled them to conquer colonies, to dominate foreign markets, and to make little England the clearing house of the world's commerce. We are supposed to be slackers, committed to the insane policy of ca'canny*, clamorous for our rights and eager only to be off to our sports and games.

Now my view is a different one. I hold that if the working classes are becoming slack and careless about their work, slack and careless, too, about their moral life, it is just because they do not play games. I hold that they are suffering from a most cruel and dangerous deprivation. They go once a week in melancholy masses to look on at games, but not one in a thousand, perhaps not one in ten thousand, ever takes off his coat, rolls up his sleeves, and plays a game with all the might of his mind behind it. Now that is an unnatural state of things for any Englishman.

The modern worker is ceasing to be an Englishman. He doesn't dance, he doesn't sing, he doesn't run, he doesn't jump, he doesn't wrestle, he doesn't box, and when he sees a ball he doesn't feel in his bones that it is his bounden duty either to hit it or to kick it.

He slouches through the leisure hours of his life with no hunger and thirst in his soul for the open air, the green fields, and the thrill of a good game.

He drinks because he is miserable, he smokes because there is nothing better to do, he backs horses because he must have some excitement to prevent him from committing suicide.

In this way, he becomes careless of his body. He reads the advertisements of quack medicines, doses his vital organs with confounded chemicals, and ends his days as the victim of some horrible and depressing disease. He has never known the glory of good health, and never felt that life is a blessing for which his thanks are due to Almighty God. How can you name such a poor craven creature an Englishman?

It is a state of things which cries aloud for reformation. England was never meant to be the stone prison of Englishmen, but their green playground.

What, then, is the remedy? Access to the field: opportunity for games. Every manufacturing city and every dark commercial town should be surrounded by playing fields. It should be made easy and cheap for the workers of every congested centre to get away from their sunless streets and their sordid surroundings, to get quickly and cheerfully away to the open country, where they may play cricket and football, tennis and croquet, bowls and rounders, and, greatest of them all, golf.

In America, golf courses for their people are as common as black-berries in Devonshire. Why shouldn't it be the same here? If Chicago is surrounded by democratic, flourishing golf courses, golf courses that pay their way, why shouldn't Birmingham, Manchester, Bradford and Newcastle have the same blessing for their work people?

Politicians are obsessed by the economic aspect of industrialism. Political economy has become a bee in their bonnets. But it is my belief that the root cause of all our troubles is the starved nature of the modern Englishman; that and nothing else; his starved nature, his unnatural social life. Politicians can only tinker with the difficulty so long as they concern themselves exclusively with hours and wages.

Capital and Labour are at strife, not because Capital gets too many of the good things in life, but because Labour gets none at all. Labour is supposed to be content with a rise in wages, grateful for an eight-hour day, satisfied by its dark home in a blighting slum so long as no profiteering landlord can kick it out or raise the rent against it. What a view to take of the Englishman.

The politicians are now going to bring peace to industrialism by means of an improved scheme of insurance. Will that humanise a slum? Will that feed a starved soul? Will that alter Labour's temper? Not for a moment. What Labour really wants, and what is absolutely necessary to its salvation, is good health and physical recreation.

Give the modern Englishman his playground and he will waste no time in listening to a tub-thumper's rehearsal of his economic wrongs and no money in feathering the nest of the political agitator. He'll save his money to buy the implement of his game, and he'll spend his time practising his game till he is perfect at it.

He'll keep clear of the public house, he won't pay near so many visits to the tobacconist, and he'll see the bookmaker in Hades before he wastes a shilling on a horse he has never seen and whose name he cannot properly pronounce. He'll find that he can do without patent medicines, and he'll discover that one of the topmost joys in life is a feeling of tremendous fitness.

Yes, and something more. He'll learn to be a good sportsman; that is to say, a fair, steady and tenacious fighter, but a good loser. He'll find himself breathing another air and looking at life from an entirely different angle. Surliness will go out of his mind, and bitterness out of his heart.

I don't set up to be a prophet, but I think I know my fellow Englishmen, and I am confident that when we are once more a nation of sportsmen, a nation of game-lovers and game-players, there'll be no more nonsensical talk of a class war, and no more crazy practising of ca'canny in our workshops and factories.

The normal Englishman, given his right and natural conditions, is neither a fool nor a traitor. He's a thundering fine fellow, but he must have health, games and good air. Those are his true and inherent rights.

No Englishman was ever meant to live as the vast majority of our people are living now. I've always hated oppression of any kind. And I say, Tory as I am and to the core of my being, the vast majority of the English nation at this moment is monstrously oppressed. Give the people playgrounds, make games easy and cheap, and economic difficulties will disappear in **❞** less than a generation, I am sure of it.

Ca'canny, in industrial terms, was a restriction of production. It comes from the Scottish word meaning to move cautiously.

THE AMERICAN
ADVENTURE

16

I T WAS very nearly the offer he couldn't refuse - a dollar-
rich deal that sorely tempted JH Taylor to abandon
Britain and start a new life in America.

Fresh from St Andrews and his third Open triumph, Taylor
travelled to the United States in August, 1900, to boost the profile
of his club-making business - his partner, George Cann, had
left Winchester two years earlier seeking to create a niche in the
lucrative market across the Atlantic.

Taylor's schedule would also include a first tilt at the US Open
title.

He had been given three months' leave of absence by Mid-Surrey,
but the trip did not start well.

The first three days of the week-long sailing from Liverpool had
been spent mostly on deck - rather than in the luxury of his first-
class cabin - because of chronic seasickness.

But events took a far healthier turn when Cann met him as
Cunard's SS Etruria docked in New York.

While Taylor was en route, Cann had been approached with a
proposition that took the trip to a whole new level - Taylor was
about to be head-hunted by one of the most famous publishing
firms in the States.

Colonel George Harvey, who later became US Ambassador to
Britain, had been recruited to revive the fortunes of Harper & Bros,
of New York, whose monthly magazine, *Golf*, broke new ground in
America. Harvey was aware that Taylor had already impressed
with contributions to other publications and, at a meeting at Deal

AMERICAN DREAM: George Cann, centre, and JH aimed to establish their club-making business in the lucrative United States market. Also photographed is Frederic George Hawtree, left

PICTURE: BATH'S PHOTOGRAPHIC

Golf Club, New Jersey, announced that he was prepared to pay JH £2,000 a year to work for him.

Taylor recalled: "It was my first introduction to the possibility of earning big money in a very pleasant manner and I readily accepted such a tempting offer. It was a gilt-edged security and we returned to New York happy in the knowledge that a good start was a very favourable sign for future prosperity."

It got better. Harper & Bros also undertook to manage and underwrite Taylor's stay in America, which relieved himself and Cann of any further financial liability for the trip.

Taylor quickly got into the swing of New York, arriving at Harper's offices in a Stetson hat "which, I fondly thought, made me look more of an American than any person on Broadway."

That may or may not have been the case, but Taylor's emphatic win over Harry Vardon at St Andrews earlier in the summer had significantly raised his marketability in the States.

However, his first public match in America, at the Deal club where he had met Colonel Harvey, was less than auspicious. Taylor, feeling extremely unwell but not wanting to disappoint the thousand or so fans who had turned out to watch, was beaten six and four in a 36-hole contest by a better-ball combination of RB Wilson and Willie Norton, two Scottish professionals working as greenkeepers in the area.

That setback aside, the tour of matches and personal appearances put together by the Harper company was so successful that Harvey and his associates came up with a new and even more staggering proposal.

They suggested that Taylor should make his home in America and that they would provide large-scale financial backing that would allow a new company, JH Taylor and Cann, to compete with the top US club-makers.

The offer had huge appeal. Taylor wrote: "Our desire to expand the business had been hampered by lack of cash. Here was the opportunity to remove that problem, possibly for ever."

Lawyers drew up a contract, but Taylor insisted on a get-out clause that the deal would terminate if he decided to return to Europe.

GEORGE CANN, JH's partner in their club-making business, had been the first to recognise the potential of gaining a foothold in the lucrative American market.

So with the "hearty approval" of his childhood friend, Cann and his new wife left Winchester at the end of 1898 to become the professional at Pittsburgh, in Pennsylvania.

Taylor wrote: "George was seized with the desire to establish a branch of the business in America, where the game was receiving one of its earliest booms. This foreshadowed not only wealth but also a greater experience - and George was always eager to gain the latter even should the acquisition of the first elude him."

It didn't quite go according to plan.

Cann, always much happier making his clubs than teaching on the practice grounds, found himself spending hours with some of the most powerful brokers in the steel business trying to educate them in the rudiments of golf.

But, as Taylor explained, there was salvation at hand: "Fortunately for his sanity and the retention of his habitual good temper, no golf was played in the winter time, so it was possible for Cann to devote his talents to what was his primary instinct, the business of club-making."

Taylor added: "It is justly due to George not to forget to record his greatest golfing triumph, the winning of the Championship of Western Pennsylvania. His modest nature would bid me to say that the competition was held on his home nine-hole course and that the opposition was not too severe, but when this is admitted it was a Championship and its winning will reflect its due glory."

Taylor recalled: "I wrote to my wife as to the possibility of her bringing our young family to join me, but like the true Briton she is, she refused absolutely to leave her native country.

"I also asked Mid-Surrey to grant me 12 months' leave of absence but, quite rightly, I think, the club refused, pointing out with justification that it could not appoint another professional in my place as a temporary stop-gap to suit me.

"The result was that at the end of my stay I claimed the protection of the operative clause and was immediately released from any further obligation, a decision that caused Cann no little disappointment.

"I admit the temptation to make my home in America was a strong one, but overriding and above all other considerations, the thought of severing myself from British golf proved even stronger and, looking back, I am glad I acted the way I did. Yes, I am more than ever convinced that I did the right and honest thing."

In the midst of all these commercial considerations, Taylor embarked on the first of his two challenges for the US Open title, at Wheaton, Illinois.

It was to be an extremely distasteful experience.

Vardon was on his second tour of the States, earning £50 a match for more than 50 challenges while also pocketing £800 from the Spalding golf company for promoting its "Vardon Flyer" golf ball.

Taylor had resisted earlier offers to play his old rival, claiming that he needed more time to acclimatise to American conditions.

By the time the pair finally squared up at Wheaton, the tournament had been billed - unreasonably, in Taylor's view - as a two-horse race between the Brits.

In fact, the pundits were correct and Vardon took the title from Taylor by two strokes with the rest of the field at least another eight shots adrift.

It wasn't the defeat that so upset Taylor, rather the "atmosphere of recrimination, from one side only, let me say" that dominated the build-up to the event.

The object of Taylor's anger, it would appear, was Vardon's US management team; he apportions no blame to Vardon himself.

Taylor recalled: "It was put about that Harry and I were deadly enemies, that he was prepared to play me for vast sums at any time and anywhere. In fact, a great deal was insinuated which was not only untrue but also positively malicious.

"It was a new experience for me, this endeavour to sow enmity between old friends and at the same time to gain illicit publicity for propaganda purposes which any decent man would abhor and repudiate."

• JH TAYLOR had travelled to the United States with an admirably persistent American entrepreneur named McMahon, who had designs on the role of self-appointed "agent" for the trip. Taylor, unconvinced, was having none of it.

The pair had been introduced at Royal Wimbledon two years earlier when McMahon asked Taylor to promote his new golf ball, the Maponite, whose main claim was that it was more durable than its competitors.

Initially, Taylor was impressed, concluding: "It combined the wear-resisting qualities of the Eclipse ball with the click of the gutty and certainly appeared to be the kind of ball the golfing world was waiting for."

McMahon already had the backing of some members of the Stock Exchange - who believed they were on to a financial killing - and when The Maponite Golf Ball Company was floated Taylor was given 200 shares for his services.

The project failed to take off - there was still a strong customer resistance to change and, unlike the gutty, it could not be "remade".

Undaunted, McMahon turned his attention to the American market. He tried to "sell" the Maponite project to Colonel Harvey, who, on the advice of Taylor and Cann, decided he wanted nothing to do with it. Taylor never saw McMahon again.

RYDER GLORY

17

JOHN HENRY TAYLOR was thrilled to be honoured with the captaincy of the Great Britain Ryder Cup team in 1933 - but, for a while, it looked as though the match might not go ahead.

According to Taylor, the drama unfolded on the eve of the match at Southport and Ainsdale, in Lancashire, when the captains were due to lodge their foursomes pairings and playing order for the singles in sealed envelopes.

Walter Hagen, the United States captain, missed two "appointments", at 3pm and 5pm, and an exasperated Taylor - with the full backing of his team - delivered an ultimatum that if he hadn't received the information by 9pm the match would be off.

It wasn't that they suspected the Americans of sharp practice, just that protocols should be observed.

The envelope duly arrived - and the crisis was averted.

It should come as no surprise that Taylor, at 62 years, three months and seven days the oldest man to lead GB's Ryder Cup challenge, would still want to bring his own innovative style to the team's preparations.

The non-playing captain broke new ground by boosting his back-up team with a fitness trainer, his friend Lt Alick Stark.

Stark's regime of pre-breakfast runs on Southport sands followed by a massage didn't exactly meet with universal acclaim at first, but everyone eventually bought into the idea, as Taylor recalled, "if not with alacrity, then with every show of docile obedience."

The tactic certainly did no harm, with a crowd of 15,000 roaring Great Britain to an enthralling 6½ -5½ victory on the final green of the last singles match still on the course.

WINNING FEELING: JH Taylor receives the Ryder Cup after Great Britain's last-green victory.
PICTURE COURTESY OF SOUTHPORT AND AINSDALE GOLF CLUB

The contest was played under a different format to today's epic battles.

From the inception of the Cup in 1927 until 1959, the schedule comprised four first-day foursomes followed by eight singles on the second day, all scheduled for a maximum of 36 holes.

Great Britain - paid 42 shillings (£2.10) a day playing expenses - went into the event with ten players, although the unfortunate Allan Dailey didn't feature in any of the matches, while the Americans used a squad of ten, including Hagen as a playing captain.

The home side took the foursomes 2½ -1½, but their rivals fought back and when the last pair on the course, Syd Easterbrook and the American Denny Shute, reached their final green the overall match was tied.

With their own game also all square and both players around 30ft from the pin in three, it looked as if it would stay that way, but Easterbrook got down in two while Shute missed a six-footer for the half.

NUMBERS GAME: The scoreboard tells the story as the plot unfolds at Southport and Ainsdale
PICTURE COURTESY OF SOUTHPORT AND AINSDALE GOLF CLUB

Great Britain had reclaimed the trophy they lost in Scioto, Ohio, two years earlier, though it would be another 24 years - including six lost to the Second World War - before they experienced the elation of that winning feeling again.

Taylor had looked on his appointment as non-playing captain as "a direct, personal compliment" and was for ever grateful to the Executive Committee of the Professional Golfers' Association for awarding him the honour.

As he lifted the Ryder trophy, he proclaimed himself "the happiest man in the Commonwealth of English-speaking nations."

TAYLOR'S TIGERS: The winning GB team, back row from left, Alf Perry, Allan Dailey, Arthur Havers, Charles Whitcombe, Syd Easterbrook and Alick Stark (fitness guru). Front row: Arthur Lacey, Alf Padgham, William Davies, JH (non-playing captain), Abe Mitchell and Percy Alliss.

PICTURE: R F RIDING, SOUTHPORT

FIRST DAY FOURSOMES, Monday June 26, 1933

GREAT BRITAIN 2½ pts   UNITED STATES 1½ pts

Percy Alliss, Charles Whitcombe	HALVED	Gene Sarazen, Walter Hagen	
Abe Mitchell, Arthur Havers	BEAT	Olin Dutra, Denny Shute	3&2
William Davies, Syd Easterbrook	BEAT	Craig Wood, Paul Runyan	1 hole
Alf Padgham, Alf Perry	LOST TO	Ed Dudley, Billy Burke	1 hole

SECOND DAY SINGLES, Tuesday June 27, 1933

GREAT BRITAIN 4 pts   UNITED STATES 4 pts

Alf Padgham	LOST TO	Gene Sarazen	6&4
Abe Mitchell	BEAT	Olin Dutra	9&8
Arthur Lacey	LOST TO	Walter Hagen	2&1
William Davies	LOST TO	Craig Wood	4&3
Percy Alliss	BEAT	Paul Runyon	2&1
Arthur Havers	BEAT	Leo Diegel	4&3
Syd Easterbrook	BEAT	Denny Shute	1 hole
Charles Whitcombe	LOST TO	Horton Smith	2&1

RESULT: GREAT BRITAIN 6½ pts   UNITED STATES 5½ pts

READ ALL ABOUT IT: The official programme for the 1933 event, priced just one shilling (5p)

DESIGNER GOLF

18

THE BRIEF was to create a course fit for a Championship - and the architects certainly didn't disappoint. Royal Birkdale remains arguably the most glittering jewel in the portfolio of Hawtree and Taylor, course designers.

Nine Opens, two Ryder Cups and a host of other A-list golf events at the world-famous Lancashire links bear indisputable testimony to the success of their vision.

Like many of his peers, John Henry Taylor had developed a keen eye for course architecture and had undertaken schemes of his own, most notably the "humps and hollows" reconstruction at his club, Mid-Surrey.

But his involvement in design work escalated dramatically through his enduring partnership and friendship with the renowned Frederic George Hawtree, the first of three generations of British golf course architects.

Between the two wars they would work on more than 100 projects - designing and building new courses and reshaping existing ones - and they also created one of the world's first all-weather driving ranges in London.

Just as he had with his friend George Cann in their club-making business, so JH struck gold in his relationship with Hawtree.

Taylor's junior by 12 years, Hawtree worked as a gardener and then a greenkeeper at Sundridge Park, Kent, before branching out into course design in 1912.

In the early days he linked up with another of the Great Triumvirate, James Braid, but the pair ended their association when some investment advice passed on to Hawtree by Braid went terribly wrong.

COURSE MANAGEMENT:
Taylor and Hawtree
worked on more than
100 projects together
after forming their design
company in 1922

Taylor and Hawtree had no such problems, formalising their partnership in 1922 with the establishment of their company, Hawtree and JH Taylor Ltd.

Martin Hawtree, Frederic's grandson and the third member of the design dynasty, said: "I believe they first met at an Open Championship. They got on very well from the start and that's probably because they had so much in common. They both came from very humble backgrounds and were both very religious. Both recognised the value of education - they sent sons to Oxford - and they also believed that golf should be available to everyone, whatever their social status."

LEVEL PLAYING FIELD: Hawtree and Taylor opted for flat fairways - this is the 13th hole at Royal Birkdale - that cut a swathe through the sand hills, rather than go over them.
PICTURE COURTESY OF ALAN C. BIRCH AND ROYAL BIRKDALE GOLF CLUB

Many of the projects they worked on were public courses and such was their commitment to the principle of golf for all that both Taylor and Hawtree were founding fathers of the National Association of Public Golf Courses and the Artisan Golfers' Association.

As managing director of the company, Hawtree took the lead role, responsible for the day-to-day details of design and construction.

Taylor's input came at early site visits and interviews with clients and, whenever his schedule allowed, he would play an exhibition match at the official opening of the new or refurbished courses.

The opportunity to shape the future of Royal Birkdale came in 1932.

The club's new landlords, Southport Corporation, had granted a 99-year lease on the understanding that the course would be upgraded to Championship standard within seven years.

Birkdale's members gave the go-ahead for the blueprint at their annual meeting in 1931 and agreed that Hawtree and J H Taylor Ltd should be offered the contract.

The club's website reports: "The initial proposal was for six completely new holes, five new greens to existing holes, four remodelled greens, 20 new tees, five new fairways and four approaches.

BEST SEAT IN TOWN: The sand hills, like these at the 12th hole, make excellent viewing points for the spectators at Royal Birkdale, the jewel in the Hawtree-Taylor portfolio.
PICTURE COURTESY OF ALAN C. BIRCH AND ROYAL BIRKDALE GOLF CLUB

"The proposals were both radical and costly and a number of modifications were suggested. Finally a compromise was reached, a figure of just under £4,000 was accepted and the contract with the architects signed in September, 1932.

"Hawtree and Taylor's philosophy was to lay out the holes in the valleys between the sand hills rather than over them. This allowed each hole to be self-contained and led, for the most part, to the avoidance of blind shots and the undulating fairways traditionally associated with links golf, thus enabling Birkdale to gain the reputation of being one of the fairest of the Championship courses.

"The exception to the general pattern was one of the entirely new holes, the ninth, which featured a blind tee shot over a sand hill.

"The architects set great store on accuracy, and bunkers were strategically placed to reinforce the not inconsiderable natural hazards. According to the specifications, bunkers were designed to punish pulled or sliced drives and second shots.

"Hawtree and Taylor designed a course that was tough but fair, with virtually flat fairways threading their way along natural valleys which lie between mighty dunes. It is a course that rewards straight shots but all too often sees a wayward shot swallowed up by the surrounding buckthorn, willow scrub and rough. The hills provide ideal natural vantage points for spectators who, in the years ahead, were to come in increasing numbers to witness a succession of major events played over the links.

"Without doubt Birkdale fulfilled its obligation by providing a world-class course. The pioneers of the 1930s could not have envisaged the phenomenal success of the course as a Championship venue. Its record for hosting major events over the last 60 years is arguably second to none and that success was initially due to the architectural skills of Hawtree and Taylor."

Royal Birkdale was scheduled to make its debut on the Open roster in 1940, but the Championship was suspended because of the war. It eventually hosted its first Open in 1954 and has since staged eight more, the most recent in 2008.

The Hawtree family has remained closely associated with Royal Birkdale for more than 70 years.

Martin's father, Frederic William, designed the new short 12th hole for the 1965 Championship, while Martin redeveloped all 18 greens in time for the 1998 Open and made further changes for 2008, tightening the greens, bringing the surrounds closer to the putting surfaces, and adding a small number of bunkers and tees.

In no small part due to the skills of its four Irish foremen, Regan, Ryan, Brick and Ward, who all had their own special talents for shaping golf courses, Hawtree and Taylor Ltd earned a first-class reputation throughout Britain and Europe until it went into voluntary liquidation just after the end of the Second World War.

The Hawtree philosophy of golf course architecture is unashamedly rooted in the history and traditions of the game. At the heart of this approach is good layout. If the layout is wrong, no amount of landscaping or publicity will put it right. The right layout will frequently save money and preserve the existing character of the site.

Once the layout is established, then is the time to focus on the detailed design - the enhancement of natural features, the strategy and fairness of play, the broader fields of landscaping and maintenance.

Not every job, though, went entirely according to plan. Frederic William recalled in the book, *Aspects of Golf Course Architecture*

174

1889-1924, how JH was called back to one club when there were complaints that it was impossible to hold the ball on one of the new short-hole greens the company had created.

Hawtree wrote: "The hole was of mashie length, Taylor's favourite iron. His ball flew gracefully from tee to green, bit the turf and stopped. There were no further complaints but there were perhaps a few lessons. . ."

THE HAWTREE-TAYLOR COURSES

AMONG the courses designed and built by Hawtree and JH Taylor Ltd are:

1921: Ipswich, Suffolk; Lickey Hills Municipal, Birmingham
1922: High Post, Wiltshire; Hollingbury Park, Sussex; Welwyn Garden City, Hertfordshire; Hilton course, Hilton Park, near Glasgow, Scotland
1923: Addington Palace, Surrey; Bigbury, Devon; Richmond Park, Surrey, public course
1925: Chigwell, Essex; Highwoods, Bexhill-on-Sea, Sussex; Knowle, Bristol; Richmond Park, Surrey, second public course
1926: Moor Woods, Birmingham; Gorleston, Suffolk; Harborne Church Farm, Birmingham; Swinton Park, Lancashire; Arklow, Co Wicklow, Ireland
1927: Ifield, Sussex
1928: Woodlands Manor, Kent; Wyke Green, Middlesex; Bastad, Sweden
1929: Pinner Hill, Middlesex; Selsdon Park Hotel, Surrey
1930: Easingwold, North Yorkshire; Rhuddlan, Clwyd, Wales
1931: Lower and Old Courses; Addington Court, Surrey; Harpenden, Herts
1932: Elfordleigh, Devon; Pype Hayes municipal, Warwickshire; White Webbs municipal, Middlesex
1935: Hill Barn, Sussex; Southampton
1936: Batchwood Hall, St Albans, Herts
1937: Rickmansworth, Herts
1938: Ruislip, Middlesex

AMONG the courses remodelled by the partnership are:

Filton, Bristol; Freshwater Bay, Isle of Wight; Hainault Forest, Essex; Henbury, Gloucestershire; Littlehampton, Sussex; Rochford Hundred, Essex; Royal Birkdale, Southport, Lancashire; Sonning, Berkshire; and West Middlesex.

JH TAYLOR had enthusiastically embraced a commission to lay out a new golf course in the Egyptian desert - never once imagining that he might be signing up to a very sandy and solitary demise.

The course was to be built at a new town, Heliopolis, five miles outside Cairo and, on his first day at work, Taylor had been dropped at the site by his driver, a British Army captain, who would return later in the day to pick him up.

Taylor wrote: "The job was a very interesting experience which I much enjoyed, but during it I received a shock that nearly frightened me to death. From the contour point of view, the desert was an ideal situation for a golf course, beautifully undulating country with not too deep folds in the ground. I strolled about getting some idea of the lie of the land and, spotting a hill higher than the rest that would give a better view, I proceeded to climb it.

"When I reached the top I came face to face with a figure that instantly turned my thoughts to my wife and children and the possibility of never seeing them again, the figure of a real Bedouin, a dirty sack around his shoulders and little else by way of covering, with a wicked double-barrelled gun as his chief armament.

"I have heard of hearts missing a beat, but mine must have missed a whole bar. As far as I could tell I was miles from anyone and the likelihood of being shot and conveniently buried did not escape my agitated mind. I had in my pocket some cigarettes and in a moment of profound inspiration offered one which, I was thankful to observe, was accepted with signs of delight."

JH also invited his "companion" to share his lunch, which, too, was eaten with relish, but he was still mighty relieved when five o'clock came and his driver finally returned.

Taylor added: "When I told him of my adventure and my fears, he roared with laughter.

"My dusky pal was engaged in the innocent task of seeing that the boundary posts were not removed and he had stalked me on the hill-top wondering if I had evil designs. He kept watch day and night, sleeping in a hole dug out of the side of a sand dune.

"My work took me three days. On the last I brought a driver along and his delight when I drove a ball gave me a thrill that more than recompensed for the fright of our first meeting. I was sorry to part from my nomad friend."

TAYLOR TITBITS

19

JH Taylor's father, Joshua, was not a golfer, but, crucially, he was a "potwalloper". As a ratepayer in the manor of Northam and Appledore, Joshua was entitled to rights of "exercise and air" on the Burrows, where the RND golf course was laid out.

"Potwallopers" - those who could "boil a pot" on their own hearth - also had another role. Around the beginning of the 17th century a huge bank of stones, famously known as the Pebble Ridge, amassed along the two-mile stretch of Westward Ho! beach, creating a natural barrier between the Atlantic ocean and the Burrows behind.

The pebbles, rounded on their journey, had formed through coastal erosion further along the cliffs towards Cornwall, and the

RIDGE RESCUE: 'Potwallopers' help to rebuild the Pebble Ridge at Westward Ho! after it had been ravaged by the winter storms   PICTURE COURTESY OF DAVID GALE

"potwallopers" met at the onset of summer to rebuild the sea defences by replacing the pebbles dislodged by the pounding winter tides. When, at the age of 15, golf club rules dictated that he could no longer be a caddie, Taylor was consoled with the knowledge that, "being the son of a potwalloper, the use of the links was mine whenever the fancy seized."

* * *

IT WAS the custom for many players at Westward Ho! to give their caddies a bottle of ginger beer to drink while the golfers took lunch. The resourceful caddies had carved out some short holes on the edge of the course to improve their pitching skills - and they used the drinks as stake money when they played against each other. JH, of course, won more than he lost - and, far from making him tire of the tipple, it remained one of the preferred refreshments of the teetotal champion.

* * *

JH and James Braid were among a group of professionals playing in Italy and had decided on a day off to visit the Coliseum in Rome. Seeing Braid's complete lack of interest, Taylor tried to lift his friend's spirits by telling him that hundreds of thousands of sight-seers made the trip to see the famous ruins. To which Braid replied: "It's a pity they don't have something better to do with their time."

* * *

TO SAVE money JH and James Braid would often share a room and occasionally, when there was an acute shortage of accommodation, the same bed - as happened during his 1900 triumph at St Andrews. Back in their room after a punishing 36 holes on the links, the pair would rub each other down with embrocation - and JH was aggrieved that, with Braid standing at 6ft2in compared with his 5ft8in frame, he had an unfair share of the workload!

* * *

"SUPPOSE your house is one fire: would you rather have Lord Balfour by your side, or James Braid? Suppose you are drifting on a raft in the midst of the Atlantic: would you rather have the Bishop of London for your companion or JH Taylor?

"Do you not feel that Braid and Taylor, whatever their moral outlook, possess a quality, lacking in the other two, which would enable them calmly and masterfully to take charge of your desperate fortunes? And, on reflection, do you not acknowledge that this supreme and superlative quality is that power of the human spirit which we call self-control - self-mastery? From *Its Moral Beauty: By a Divotee*, published by Mills and Boon in 1923

* * *

TAYLOR didn't just grace golf's great courses - he actually took a wicket at Lord's playing for a team of "Cricketing Golfers" against the "Golfing Cricketers". The none-too-serious match, in aid of the PGA Benevolent Fund, ended in a draw.

* * *

THERE was no triumphant return to Westward Ho! for JH in 1920. Rounds of 74, 72, 74 and 81 left him in third place, ten shots adrift of the winner, George Duncan, in the *Daily Mail* tournament.

* * *

"TAYLOR is well-liked and respected, both by the amateurs who know him and by his brother professionals. It is only a pity that we no longer have a Kingsley to do justice to a Devon hero so worthy of his eulogy" - Horace Hutchinson writing in *Golf* magazine in 1894.

* * *

WHEN his daughter, Phyllis, returned home from school each afternoon, JH would sit down with her and ask what she had learned that day. He was not putting her to the test to see if she had absorbed the lessons correctly - he simply wanted to increase the knowledge he had lost by having to leave school so early.

* * *

JH twice suffered the indignity of falling foul of the law on his travels. While in France for his golfing "tour" with the Aga Khan he was fined 145 francs for unwittingly trying to take too much currency out of the country - his host paid the fine for him - while on a train trip from Genoa to Ventimiglia in Italy he and his pals were rebuked by police for playing ha'penny nap. Apparently, it was against the law to play cards in a public place.

* * *

GOLF magazine, 1898: "Winning or losing, there is an ease and a snap about Taylor's play that is very captivating to watch and he plays with a dash and concentration which is in striking contrast to the more deliberate methods of most other players."

IN 1957, JH Taylor gave RND 36 original water-colour sketches - painted under the pseudonym of "Shortspoon" by Major Hopkins - that he had bought for £25 when the Union Club in Westward Ho! closed down. The paintings were lost to the club for 11 years, were returned in 1983 - then some were resold to help pay for a new watering system and clubhouse refurbishment. Quite a result from a local caddie boy who would not even have been allowed in the clubhouse in his early days!

* * *

THE celebrated golf writer and commentator, Henry Longhurst, upset Taylor when he complained that he had to pay 35 shillings (£1.75) for a driver that did not compare with its American equivalent. JH retorted that he had never charged more than a guinea (£1.05) for any of his clubs - and they were every bit as good as their US rivals.

* * *

"TAYLOR told me he was so nervous all through the meeting (the 1900 Open) that he hardly had a wink of sleep, and he was also unable to eat. If the proprietors of Bovril want an advertisement, I advise them to apply to the Open champion, for he told me it was chiefly on that preparation that he accomplished his marvellous performance" - *Golf Illustrated*, 1900

* * *

JH shot ten holes-in-one during his career.

* * *

THE Royal Mid-Surrey Committee decided on March 16, 1901, that Taylor should be allowed to charge a teaching fee of five shillings (25p) per round, or 3s-6d (17.5p) for an hour. Taylor frequently chaired the club's Greens Committee and occasionally sat on the Finance Committee, but he was not involved when the club proposed that "the green fees paid by a gentleman member introducing a lady shall be the same as that payable by a lady introducing a gentleman, viz five shillings".

* * *

IN THE aftermath of the 1926 General Strike, JH wrote to *The Times* urging all golf clubs, particularly those in the Metropolitan area and the Home Counties, to offer playing concessions to the police "to partially repay the debt of gratitude" to them for their service

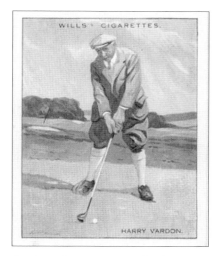

during the unrest. "Such a concession would be productive of much good," he wrote. "The clubs would enrol a force that would take a great interest in the welfare of the course; and they would be giving to a loyal body of men means of pleasant recreation that many of them have no opportunity of enjoying."

* * *

YOU knew that you had arrived at the top of your profession when you featured on cigarette cards - and JH, top right, was no exception. Originally blank and used as stiffeners for the packaging, the cards sprang up in America in the 1870s as marketing tools. British companies like WD and HO Wills and John Player adopted the trend, with the day's leading sportsmen soon becoming a popular choice for collectors. JH obviously fitted this description, but it didn't prevent the non-smoking champion from airing the opinion that the habit was bad for the health of the nation.

* * *

WHEN, in his mid-80s, JH was asked to be president of Royal North Devon for 1957, he was at first hesitant about accepting. "You see," he told one of his sons, "they play so much golf on a Sunday I just can't be there and sing in the choir at matins and evensong." His son assured him he wouldn't be expected to be at the club every Sunday, so he accepted.

IN JANUARY, 1915, the secretary at Mid-Surrey was instructed to accept Speckley-Smith's estimate of three pounds 15 shillings (£3.75) to rebuild the chimney stack of JH's house.

* * *

SHORTLY before Mid-Surrey's annual meeting on January 24, 1914, JH was presented with a testimonial subscribed by members to celebrate his fifth Open Championship victory - his third with the club - at Hoylake the previous summer.

THE THOUGHTS OF JH ON. . .

THE POPULARITY OF GOLF: "The great period of the game's expansion was between 1888-1894 when the English, slow on the uptake, realised that it was a game, at once healthy and purposeful, especially suited for the middle-aged and elderly, to take the place of other and more strenuous exercises. During this time the game recovered what may be described as its second wind. Courses sprang up all over the country. It became the fashion to play golf, and like lots of other instances when fashion led, it swept through the land with an irresistible urge."

THE PSYCHE OF GOLF: "Assure yourself that golf is 95 per cent mental and only a miserable, contemptible and measly five per cent physical."

THE VALUE OF A CHAMPION: "Get it out of your head that only a champion knows the full bliss of golf. A champion is useful simply because he raises the standard. He prevents the 18-handicap man from being self-satisfied and the four-handicap man from being conceited. That is the purpose of all excellence."

THE CLARET JUG (right): "A most insignificant pot, by the way."

CLUB-MAKING: "The combination of good player and club-maker was a valuable asset in securing a post. Even now, I dread to think of the terrible hash I used to make of the simple repairs that came my way at Burnham."

BOXING AND GOLF: "Much the same strategy is employed in both contests: the finding out of the weak spots of an opponent in the early rounds, or holes, culminating in the rush at the finish when well-directed blows count and strokes are made to discomfort."

CADDIES: "The young caddie is the most discerning creature. He will readily respond to kind and humane treatment and give of his best in return, but once his susceptibilities are aroused the player may expect, if not open hostility, a grudging and unsatisfactory service. The caddie has a way of getting his own back."

WESTWARD HO!: "I doubt whether Charles Kingsley's celebrated and romantic novel, *Westward Ho!*, would have done the trick of putting the place in the category it is today (1943) had not the links greatly helped its fame and probably enhanced the book's sales and well-deserved popularity. The novel gave it the name, but the links established its fame as one of the most natural and testing seaside golfing adventures in the country."

THE ULTIMATE TEST: "The winning of The Open saps the vitality to a far greater extent than is commonly supposed and demands that none but the fit, strong, courageous and most skilful golfer can ever hope to be suc-cessful."

A SOGGY DAY AT PRESTWICK: "I played the second round (in 1893) in a downpour that soon dampened my spirits, soaking me to the skin beside obliterating my chances. In those days, our wooden clubs were faced with leather and, playing with the hard gutty ball, the hitting surface was reduced to pulp. It was like trying to hit the ball with a bundle of faggots."

EDUCATION: "The longer I went to school the more it was borne in my mind that education did not only mean that one should be fully conversant with the Three Rs. Education in itself can carry one only a little way in the world, but if one can grasp its vital meaning and apply it to everyday life, it is all-conquering."

DEVONSHIRE HEROES: "The names of Raleigh, Hawkins, Grenville, Frobisher and Drake are an inspiration to all true Devonians and I count myself as one of Devon's most loyal sons."

THE JOYS OF 1909: "The previous autumn I had won the *News of the World* Match Play tournament, so at the time of my second success in France I was the holder of the Open and French Open Championships, the *News of the World* competition and the proud father of twin girls. Surely a sufficiency of glory and more than enough to satisfy the most ambitious."

MAN OF HONOURS

20

E MADE history as an honorary member of The Royal and Ancient Golf Club of Andrews, his memory is perpetuated in stained glass windows in his local church, he even has a road and golf course named after him. . .

The life and achievements of John Henry Taylor have been honoured in a myriad of ways both before and since his death in February, 1963.

Arguably the most prestigious recognition of his services to the game of golf came in 1950 when JH, his fellow "member" of the Great Triumvirate James Braid and another Scot, Willie Auchterlonie, became the first golf professionals to be conferred with honorary life membership of The Royal and Ancient club.

The feats of Taylor and Braid are well documented, those of Auchterlonie perhaps less so to the average fan. A son of St Andrews, at 21 years and 24 days he was the second youngest Open winner when he claimed his only Championship in 1893. He began his working career as an apprentice club-maker, ran his own business for much of his life and for many years was honorary professional at his home-town club.

The three ground-breakers were considered for membership because of their considerable playing achievements and their impeccable character, but it was not a decision that The Royal and Ancient Club took without great deliberation - and it had to be unanimous, as these fascinating minutes reveal:

01 May, 1950 - General Committee:

Letter from Colonel Inglis suggesting Braid, Taylor and Auchterlonie be made Honorary Members of the Club. It was

The Royal & Ancient Golf Club
of St. Andrews, Fife.

18th September, 1950

Dear Sir,

In view of your long and distinguished services to the game of Golf and being desirous of honouring you for them the General Committee of the Royal and Ancient Golf Club have decided unanimously to invite you to accept the Honorary Life Membership of the Club.

The addition of your name to this illustrious list will be a recognition by golfers the world over of your genius and service to Golfers not only in this Country but throughout the world.

The Captain has extended the invitation by telegram and I append an extract from the Rules of the Club on the subject :~

"VII. Honorary Members. The General Committee shall be empowered to invite Princes of the Blood-Royal or other distinguished strangers to become Honorary Members of the Club, subject to the approval and confirmation of the first General Meeting after such invitation. Honorary Members shall not pay entrance money or subscription and shall have no vote in the Club affairs."

Yours faithfully,

J. A. S. CARSON.

Secretary.

J. H. Taylor, Esq. 23 Windmill Lane, Northam, Devon

HISTORY MAN: This is the letter from The Royal and Ancient Golf Club of St Andrews in 1950 in which JH was informed he was being made an honorary member of the club - along with James Braid and Willie Auchterlonie they were the first professional golfers to be awarded such an accolade

185

agreed that nothing could be done in this connection until the Rule on Honorary Members had been redrafted.

14 August, 1950 - General Committee:

In discussion about new Rules - In connection with the Rule regarding the election of Honorary Members, Lord Balfour of Burleigh enquired what the procedure would be if the Committee desired to invite Messrs W. Auchterlonie, J. Braid and J.H. Taylor to become Honorary Members. The Committee came to the conclusion that the word 'stranger' in the existing Rule applies to any person who is not a member of the Club and that these gentlemen would therefore be eligible under the old Rules. Lord Balfour of Burleigh expressed himself as strongly in favour of inviting these gentlemen to become Honorary Members and stated the arguments in favour of doing so. He was conscious, however, of the possible danger of creating a precedent and he was anxious that the invitation, if extended at all, should be unanimous. He said that he would sound those members of the Committee who were not present and would bring the matter up at the Meeting of the Committee on 18th September for final decision.

18 September, 1950 - General Committee:

The Captain moved that invitations be issued to Messrs W. Auchterlonie, J. Braid and J.H. Taylor to become Honorary Life Members of the Club. He emphasised the fact that he did so in view of their long and distinguished records and high personal characters, but even so would only have thought it right to proceed in the matter if there was complete unanimity in the Committee. He suggested that, as this case might in future be quoted as precedent, the Committee should record their opinion that such complete unanimity was essential. Sir George Cunningham seconded the proposal. The Committee agreed unanimously that invitations be immediately sent to these three gentlemen in view of their notable golfing careers, their great contribution to the game of golf, and their high personal qualities, and that the Chairman should place the matter before the General Meeting.

19 September, 1950 - Business meeting:

Wethered announced the invitation to Auchterlonie, Braid and Taylor to become Honorary Life Members of the Club. This was greeted with acclamation. Balfour then pointed out that the list of Honorary Members of this Club is an illustrious one, embracing as it does members of the Royal Family, distinguished Americans and other celebrities, and that Honorary Membership had never before been conferred on a Professional and it was possible it may never happen again. The General Committee, he said, felt that the three gentlemen invited were worthy of the honour and that the Club would be the richer by the addition of these three distinguished names. He informed the meeting that he had visited Willie Auchterlonie at his house the previous evening to extend the invitation and had received telegrams from the other two and that all three greatly appreciated the honour which had been done them and accepted the invitation.

GLASS ACT: Two of the stained glass windows sponsored by the golf authorities in memory of JH Taylor at St Margaret's Church, Northam. The third was funded by The Royal and Ancient Golf Club of St Andrews

JOHN HENRY was a committed Christian who was still singing in the choir of his home church in Northam until a few years before his death.

So when, over 30 years later, St Margaret's, Northam, needed urgent repairs to its stained glass windows, the golfing fraternity was again quick to honour the memory of one of its most celebrated elder statesmen.

The Royal and Ancient Golf Club of St Andrews, the Professional Golfers' Association and the English Golf Union, together with the Artisan Golfers' Association, all agreed to sponsor restoration work to three of the windows.

Bob Trickey, then churchwarden at St Margaret's, said: "The windows needed to be remade with new lead. I thought it would be a good idea to perpetuate the memory of JH by inviting the golf authorities to pay for the work to be done.

"I was delighted that they all agreed without hesitation and they were all represented at the re-dedication service at the church in September, 1997."

Each window has a plaque beneath it. The R&A Club's tribute

SILVER TRIBUTE: The Communion chalice in this picture was one of two presented to St Margaret's Church, Northam, in 1964 by the Artisan Golfers' Association in memory of JH, who died a year earlier reads: "The remaking of this window in 1997 was sponsored by The Royal and Ancient Golf Club of St Andrews and is dedicated to perpetuate the memory of JH Taylor, a world champion golfer and chorister of his church."

The PGA commemorates "a founder member, Open champion, John Henry Taylor", while the English Golf Union and Artisan Golfers' Association plaque remembers a "world Open champion golfer and founder member of the AGA."

Another plaque, placed behind the pews where JH used to sing in the choir, reads: "This tablet commemorates the gift of two silver Communion chalices to this church in the year 1964 by The Artisan Golfers' Association in memory of John Henry Taylor, churchman, champion golfer and native of this parish."

It wasn't just the golf authorities who recognised JH's achievements.

In 1992, the local council in Northam named a road in a new housing development after him. JH's granddaughter, Judith Plumtree, suggested "JH Taylor Drive" because of its golfing

ROAD TO GLORY: The memory of JH lives on at a housing estate in his home town of Northam

189

connotation and the then Mayor of Northam, Mr. Bill Badcock, carried out the official naming ceremony.

The honours continue to come even to this day. Almost exactly 100 years after JH began a major redesign of the Outer Course at Royal Mid-Surrey, the club that he served as club professional for 47 years officially renamed it "The JH Taylor Course" in 2010.

JH would have accepted all accolades with equal grace and modesty, but Bob Trickey, a fellow church member at St Margaret's, has no doubts about which award meant most to his friend. He said: "I knew JH well and he told me he considered the offer to be president of Royal North Devon Golf Club in 1957 as the greatest honour he had ever received."

OFF TO A TEE: The new markers for the JH Taylor course at Royal Mid-Surrey Golf Club
PICTURE COURTESY OF ROYAL MID-SURREY GOLF CLUB

1894:   Open champion, Royal St George's Golf Club, Sandwich
1895:   Open champion, Royal and Ancient Golf Club of St Andrews
1900:   Open champion, St Andrews
1901:   Founded the Professional Golfers' Association and elected first chairman
1908:   French Open champion
1909:   Open champion, Royal Cinque Ports, Deal. Captain of the PGA (as Open champion). French Open champion
1912:   German Open champion
1913:   Open champion, Royal Liverpool Golf Club, Hoylake. Captain of the PGA (as Open champion)
1920:   Made an honorary member of Royal Mid-Surrey Golf Club
1921:   Founded Artisan Golfers' Association and elected vice president
1923:   Chairman of the PGA
1925:   Made honorary life member of the Priory Golf Club, renamed the Richmond Park Golf Club in 1953. Presented with desk and chair by the Artisan Golfers' Association as "a mark of esteem".

SHAKE ON IT:
JH, left, and the
US Ryder Cup
captain,
Walter Hagen
before the
match in 1933

1926:   Made honorary member of Royal North Devon Golf Club
1927:   Founded National Association of Public Golf Courses. Made
        honorary life member of Burnham and Berrow Golf Club
1933:   Captained Britain's Ryder Cup team in win over USA
1934:   Made president of the Artisan Golfers' Association
1936:   Chairman of the PGA
1945:   Made a life member of Royal Mid-Surrey
1948:   Made life member of Northam Golf Club, formerly the Northam
        Working Men's Golf Club
1949:   Elected a vice-president of the Professional Golfers' Association.
        Made honorary member of Royal Winchester Golf Club.
        Presented with a portrait in oils by the committee and members
        of Royal North Devon
1950:   Made an honorary life member of The Royal and Ancient Golf
        Club of St Andrews. The invitation quoted the club rule that
        empowers the committee to extend the offer to "Princes of the
        Blood Royal and other distinguished strangers"
1952:   Made president of the National Association of Public Golf
        Courses. Held that position for four years
1955:   Presented with a scroll bearing the signatures of 150
        of America's senior professionals as a tribute to "one of
        golf's immortals"
1957:   Made president of Royal North Devon and president of Royal
        Birkdale Golf Club.
1961:   On his 90th birthday, he was presented with a gold and silver
        salver inscribed with "admiration and affection" and bearing the
        signatures of the then captain and former holders of that office
        at The Royal and Ancient Golf Club of St Andrews
1964:   Artisan Golfers' Association presented two silver Communion
        chalices to St Margaret's Church, Northam, in memory of JH
1975:   Inducted into the World Golf Hall of Fame in its lifetime
        achievement category
1983:   Voted one of three outstanding golfers of the century in the
        Whitbread British Sports Awards
1992:   Road on a new housing estate in his home village of Northam
        named "JH Taylor Drive" in his honour
1997:   The Royal and Ancient Golf Club of St Andrews, the Professional
        Golfers' Association, the Artisan Golfers' Association and the
        English Golf Union sponsor the remaking of three stained glass
        windows in St Margaret's Church, Northam, in his memory
2010:   Royal Mid-Surrey renamed its "Outer" course "The JH Taylor
        Course"

UNITED IN TRIBUTE: Around 150 PGA Seniors of America signed this commendation to "one of golf's immortals" in 1955. The citation to John Henry from some of the greatest names in US golf expressed "the highest esteem and affection from your many friends in America for the great part you have played in this glorious, royal and ancient game of golf"

THE FINAL FAREWELL

21

A PRIVATE man whose prodigious talent thrust him into the most public of arenas. A champion golfer who championed the people's right to golf. A proud Devonian who made Devon proud.

The end to an extraordinary life came on February 10, 1963, when John Henry Taylor - golf professional for 56 years, five times Open champion and a passionate crusader for the cause of golf for the working classes - passed away at his home in Northam 37 days short of his 92nd birthday.

A journey that began by pony and trap in 1891 had taken in France, Germany, Austria, Switzerland, Sweden, Italy, the United States, Canada, South Africa and Egypt as well as the length and breadth of Great Britain and Ireland.

It finished in the village where it all started, in the parish church of St Margaret's where he had sung in the choir as a boy and again, in retirement, until a few years before his death.

The world of golf arrived to pay homage to a truly remarkable man.

Representatives of The Royal and Ancient Golf Club of St Andrews, the Professional Golfers' Association, the Artisan Golfers' Association and the National Association for Public Golf Courses joined family, friends and other members of the golfing fraternity as they paid their final respects at his funeral.

The vicar of Northam, the Rev Michael Lucas, told the congregation: "We hear a great deal about amateurs and professionals in sport and we also hear a great deal about gentlemen and players. JH is being remembered widely as one of the

FAREWELL: St Margaret's Church, Northam, where the golfing fraternity, family and friends gathered for the funeral of John Henry Taylor in February 1963. He is buried in the church cemetary where his wife Clara, beloved mother Susannah, and father Joshua are also laid to rest.

great golf professionals - and we in Northam remember him as a great Christian gentleman."

JH's life-long achievements were honoured later in the year at a memorial service in St Martin-in-the-Fields, London.

Lord Brabazon of Tara, then president of the Professional Golfers' Association, said in his address: "As long as the game of golf is played in every country in the world, the name of John Henry Taylor will be remembered. He was the first Englishman to become an Open champion golfer. He it was who, by setting a standard of uprightness and honesty, raised the status of the professional golfer in society. He founded the PGA and was its first chairman.

HE WAS 'ONE OF GOLF'S IMMORTALS'

Mr. J. H. Taylor, of Northam, dies at 91

WORLD-WIDE messages of sympathy and tribute have this week poured into Northam, to the home of Mr. John Henry Taylor, "one of golf's immortals," who died there on Sunday. He would have been 92 on March 19th.

His home—"Wavertree," Windmill Lane, where in latter years he was cared for by a daughter, Mrs. P. Plumtree—overlooks the Royal North Devon golf club course where he learned the rudiments of a game that was to take him to the pinnacle of fame.

The son of a labourer and entering the game as a caddie, he was to achieve fame in his early twenties, fortune and the distinction of having his company sought by some of the highest in this and other lands.

well as on the Continent on innumerable occasions.

WITH PRINCES

Among those with whom the game brought him into contact were King Edward VIII and King George V before their accessions. He played with W. G. Grace the famous cricketer and was presented with original drawings of himself by Punch famous artists Sir Bernard Partridge and Frank Reynolds and a poem by Sir Owen Seaman, a former editor of Punch.

In his lifetime he holed in one on 10 occasions.

Mr. Taylor married at Bideford Parish Church on April 17th, 1895. Miss Clara Fulford, youngest daughter of the late Mr. and Mrs. J. Fulford. They celebrated their diamond wedding in 1955. Mrs. Taylor died the following year.

Honours continued to fall to Mr. Taylor long after retirement. Perhaps the greatest came in 1950 when he was

TRIBUTE: JH's local newspaper, the *Bideford Gazette*, reports his passing in February, 1963

"Mr Taylor will be remembered, however, not only as a golfer but as a man of strong and resolute character, unspoilt by success, whose manners were impeccable and who, although humble, would fight hard for a principle or to help his less fortunate friends in the profession.

"His gentle courtliness never varied towards royalty or the most humble of his friends. And now we are gathered to say farewell to one of the very few people we meet in the world who could be called a really great man."

Bernard Darwin wrote an introduction for JH's autobiography, published 19 years before his death. The words he used then are just as fitting now.

"It saddens me," Darwin wrote, " to think that many people will read this book who never saw JH play when he was in his pomp. They have not seen what I hold to be the most exciting spectacle that golf in my time has had to offer: JH with his cap pulled well down and his feet planted as two rocks defying an angry sea, hitting the ball with a venomous grunt into the teeth of a gale. . .

"There are two sentences in the book which I love, because they come from the depths of the writer's soul. 'I like', he says, 'to see a player settle down to his job with determination and have little patience with those who enter upon it in the spirit of a picnic. To try to play golf really well is far from being a joke, and light-hearted-ness of endeavour is a sure sign of eventual failure'.

"There stands the man revealed. JH never could or would take the game light-heartedly. He fought the enemy, he fought himself, he fought the very fates, and from this triple fray emerged triumphant. . .

"When he was playing he could concentrate his attention on his task with unexampled ferocity, but he has never thought only of himself and his own game. He has been for years the leader of his profession and he has led it to a position that would once have been deemed unattainable. Others have helped the upward trend, but I take leave to say that the situation of the golf professional today as a much respected and self-respecting person is due, far more than to any other man, to John Henry Taylor.

"He has always had sympathy for those less well off than himself. The institution of the Professional Golfers' Association, with its

Benevolent Fund, the encouragement of working men's golf clubs and the increase in public courses represent three branches of a movement into which he has thrown all his formidable energies. Since he cannot say how much they owe him, I will say it for him, whether he likes it or not."

At the age of 90, JH was asked the inevitable question about the reasons for his longevity. He replied: "Sobriety and contentedness with my environment."

John Henry Taylor had felt the cold chill of poverty and had never forgotten it.

But perhaps with that "contentedness" came a justifiable warm glow that no man could have done more to achieve the ultimate goal in his life. . . to repay the sacrifices made by his father and mother.

Golf, family, the church and honouring a debt. . . they were all his life's work.

TERRIFIC TWOSOME: John Henry and wife Clara in their later years

ROUND IN 90: JH
still keeps his hand in
as he joins the
nonagenarian club

HOLD THAT POSE: Royal
North Devon club steward
Philip Andrews, left, and
John Henry in 1938

ACKNOWLEDGEMENTS

*THE Royal North Devon Golf Club would like to thank the following for
their enthusiastic and invaluable support for this project - without them it
would not have been possible to publish this book:*

All the Taylor family, but in particular Judith Plumtree,
Roger Plumtree and John Taylor
The R&A and The Royal and Ancient Golf Club of St Andrews,
in particular Peter Dawson, Peter N Lewis, Angela Howe and
Hannah Fleming
The Professional Golfers' Association, in particular
Phil Weaver and David Wright
Peter Alliss
Patrick Cunningham and The Artisan Golfers' Association
Ken Whiteway, Ed Mitchell and The National Association of
Public and Proprietary Golf Courses/Clubs
Martin Hawtree
Mark Evans and his team at Royal North Devon Golf Club
Peter Foord, Chris Yelloly and The Royal Mid-Surrey Golf Club
Andrew Buck and Royal Winchester Golf Club, Michael Blight
and Burnhan and Berrow Golf Club, and Norman Smith and
Royal Wimbledon Golf Club
Mark Vanner and Southport and Ainsdale Golf Club
Mike Gilyeat, Royal Birkdale Golf Club, and Alan C. Birch
Alan Falkner
Amanda Fletcher
Tom Branton
Mike Stanford, Graham Wilson and Jon Dolan
The *Surrey Comet* newspaper
David Normoyle and Nancy Stulak of the USGA Museum
Philip Truett
Lewis Andrews
Bob Trickey
Edward Gaskell and the staff at Lazarus Press, Bideford